85—

# HELICONIA

*Heliconia bella* from Panama.

# HELICONIA

## AN IDENTIFICATION GUIDE

Fred Berry and W. John Kress

Smithsonian Institution Press

Washington and London

Edited by John Farrand, Jr.

Designed by Linda McKnight.

Library of Congress Cataloging-in-Publication Data
Berry, Frederick H., 1927–
    Heliconia: An Identification Guide / Fred Berry and
W. John Kress.
        p.  cm.
    Includes index.
    ISBN 1-56098-006-0 (cloth).—ISBN 1-56098-007-9
(paper)
        1. Heliconia.    2. Heliconia—Identification.
    3. Heliconia—Pictorial works.    I. Kress, W.
    John.    II. Title.
    SB413.H44B47   1991
        635.9'3421—dc20                             90-9867
British Library Cataloging-in-Publication Data is
available.

Printed in Hong Kong by South China Printing
Company, not at government expense

5   4

97   96

∞ The paper used in this publication meets the mini-
mum requirements of the American Standard for
Permanence of Paper for Printed Library Materials
Z39.48-1984.

For permission to reproduce the illustrations appearing
in this book or for information on contributors, please
correspond directly with the authors.

Pictured on the cover is *Heliconia pastazae* from Ecuador.

# Table of Contents

# Preface

*Gilbert S. Daniels*
*Indianapolis, Indiana*

Heliconias are remarkable plants, not only for the beauty of their flowers, but also for the fact that so little is known about them. Anyone traveling in the tropics cannot fail to notice these large and very conspicuous plants when they are in bloom. Although heliconias are native only to Central and South America and some of the islands of the South Pacific, their easy growth and brilliant show have made them favorite garden subjects throughout the tropics of the world. However, their size and abundance may be the very reasons why they have not been studied and described in any detail until recently. To the natives of the regions where they occur naturally, their abundance leads them to be considered as weeds and thus not worthy of attention, and to the scientist their large size has made them difficult to collect and preserve during any general collecting expedition.

All this is now changing. In 1985, the Heliconia Society International was founded. Since that time, enthusiasts for all aspects of heliconia interest have been exchanging information. In recent years, heliconias have finally come into their own horticulturally. They have become increasingly popular as landscaping plants in the tropical and subtropical regions of the world, and also as potted plants and cut flowers in those regions where they cannot be grown in the garden.

With this new popularity has come the need to identify the many species and cultivars which one may encounter. As their study has been sparse, so too has been the literature describing them, and the lack of any popular illustrated work has been particularly limiting.

I first met John Kress when he was a young graduate student and I was working on a *Heliconia* flora of Costa Rica. He joined one of my regular forays into the countryside and in a matter of a few days was introduced to most of the *Heliconia* taxa of Costa Rica. Since then he has completed his doctoral studies and gone on to join the staff of the Smithsonian Institution. He has become the world authority on the taxonomy of the genus, not only studying plants in the herbarium and the laboratory, but traveling the world over to any place where a *Heliconia* has been known to grow.

My friendship with Fred Berry came with the formation of the Heliconia Society International. Along with John and other enthusiasts, first from southern Florida, and eventually from around the world, this group provided a resource for all the extant knowledge of the genus. Fred is the absolute enthusiast. As a collector of living plants and a grower of *Heliconia*, he has amassed an unbeatable knowledge of where to find the species and how to grow them in the garden.

Fred and John together are the ultimate source for information on *Heliconia*, and with the publication of the guide on *Heliconia*, the authoritative work on the genus which has been so sorely lacking has finally come into being. Fred Berry and John Kress have produced the basic reference work that has been needed by both amateurs and professionals working with, or simply enjoying, these wonderful plants. While initially conceived as an identification guide for the cultivated taxa of *Heliconia*, this work has ended up as a great deal more. There is little sense in repeating the table of contents here, but suffice it to say that whatever you want to know about *Heliconia*, you will find it here.

# INTRODUCTION

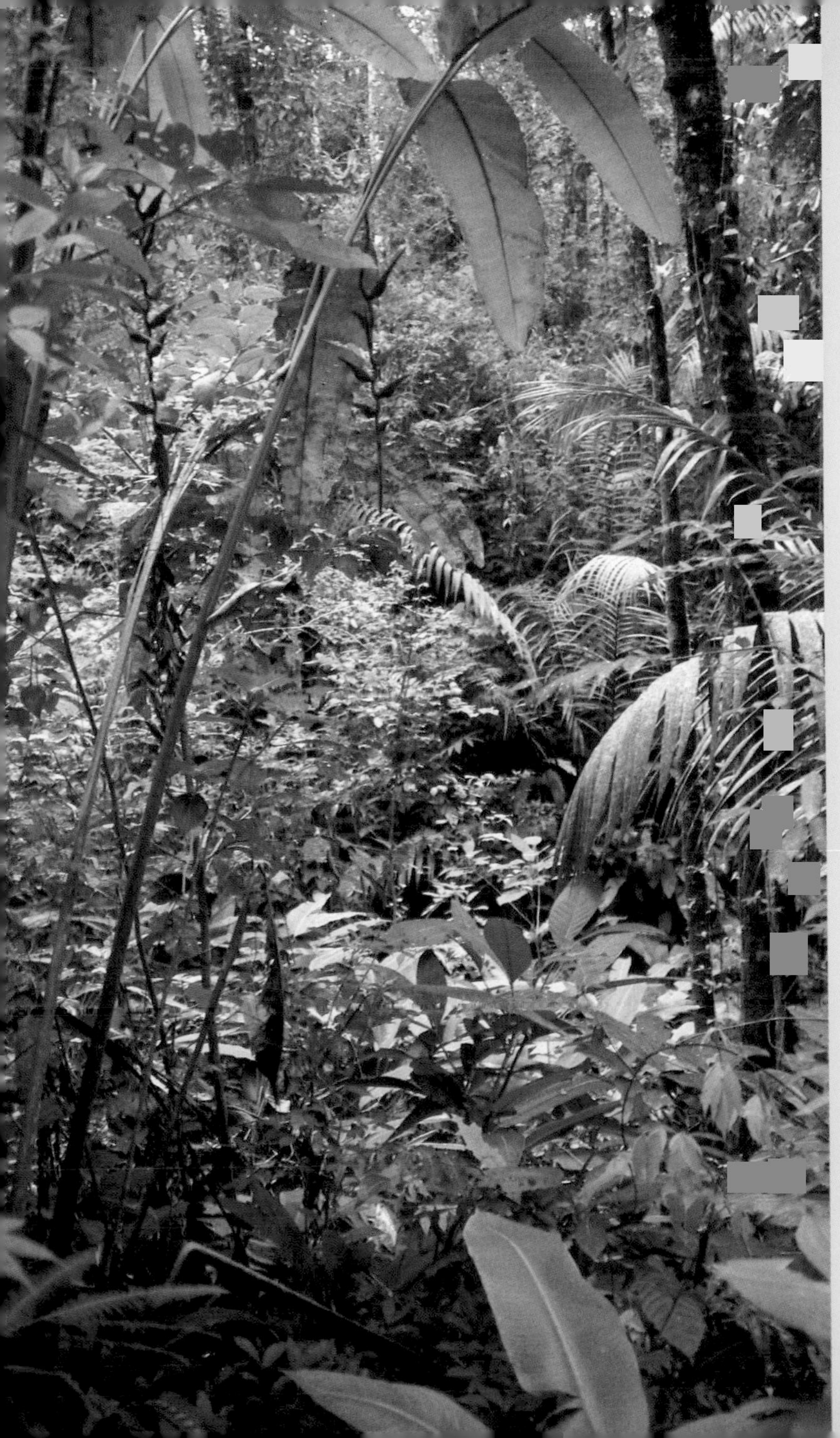

# Purpose and Scope of This Guide

During the last five years, there has emerged a renewed appreciation of and interest in the horticultural potential of the tropical heliconias. Not since Victorian times have plantsmen and the public alike shown such concern and curiosity for exotic tropical species as cut flowers, potted plants, and landscape ornamentals.

Yet except for a few recent technical works published in scholarly journals on the taxonomy of *Heliconia*, little information on these plants is available to the horticulturist and interested lay person. Standard ornamental plant texts, such as *Tropica, Exotica, Hortus Third*, and the *RHS Dictionary of Gardening*, are outdated and inadequate for the person currently interested in *Heliconia* (see "Correct Names for Heliconias Listed in Other Horticultural Publications"). With the recent introduction of dozens of new species and cultivars into public gardens, private homes, and the commercial market, correct identifications are often impossible with the current literature.

The purpose of *Heliconia: An Identification Guide* is to fill this void in the availability of information on these plants. The guide is primarily an identification manual. Correct identification of heliconias has always been a problem to professional taxonomists, horticulturists, and amateurs. Taxonomists have relied primarily on technical written descriptions and dried scientific specimens for making identifications. These sources of information are often confusing and few are available to nonspecialists. For *Heliconia,* color photographs of inflorescences and flowers are the best and easiest means of identification. Hence the objective of this guide is to provide the amateur and professional a source for easy and efficient identification of species and cultivars of *Heliconia* with photographs.

The second aim of the guide is to be a vehicle through which the great diversity of color and form found in *Heliconia* can be illustrated. Two hundred species, varieties, hybrids, and cultivars are presented here. However, there are at least that many additional forms of *Heliconia* not included in this first edition of the guide. In fact many new taxa are yet to be discovered in their native tropical habitats.

The third purpose of the guide is to help stabilize the names applied to different forms of heliconias. Many of the same plants are being brought into cultivation under different names, both horticultural and botanical. We have made a concerted effort to talk to researchers, collectors, growers, and sellers about names and we offer the 200 names in this guide for stabilized usage.

A fourth purpose is to assemble under a single cover basic information on the botany and horticulture of *Heliconia.* Many topics, including morphology, taxonomy, cultivation, commercial production, and conservation, are addressed. We hope that this information will provide the reader with a general appreciation of many different aspects of *Heliconia* not commonly provided in other books or articles.

Finally, and maybe most importantly, the purpose of this guide is to try to convey to the reader our excitement, admiration, and passion for these tropical wonders called heliconias. We have devoted much time to seeking out new heliconias in their native habitats, growing them in our gardens, studying them, and distributing them around the world. As a result of these activities we have learned much about these plants and now feel compelled to share it with others. This guide is written for people with widely different backgrounds and is intended to stimulate interest in the great diversity of nature, in this case represented by *Heliconia*. It is written for amateurs and professionals, for botanists and horticulturists, for scientists and naturalists, for tradesmen and hobbyists, and especially for all of those friends who share our obsession for these plants.

The urgent need for this guide is highlighted by the impending destruction of tropical forests around the globe. The accelerating rates of tropical deforestation caused by economic, social, and political turmoil in the developing world will certainly lead to the extinction of many species of plants and animals. This guide is intended to increase the appreciation of tropical heliconias as well as to amplify an awareness of the precarious existence of their native habitats. One can no longer admire and appreciate these plants without recognizing the biological catastrophe that threatens them and us. The ultimate purpose of the guide is to heighten this awareness.

The heart of this guide is the 200 illustrations and descriptions of species, varieties, hybrids, and cultivars of *Heliconia* (see "Names and Taxonomy" for definitions of these categories). The 89 species, 10 hybrids, and 101 varieties and cultivars that are included make this work the largest compendium of information on *Heliconia* ever assembled. The plants illustrated here were chosen primarily because they are the species and cultivars currently in cultivation. Almost all of them are available from at least one commercial nursery. In some cases, we have included plants that are not now widely cultivated, but in our opinion have significant horticultural promise. In other cases, species were selected because they are common in their native habitat and likely to be encountered by collectors, or because they are exceedingly rare.

The treatment for each plant includes verified botanical and horticultural names, a color photograph of the inflorescence, and a brief description of morphological features, blooming time, habitat, and geographic distribution. The botanical names are based on published reports by taxonomic specialists (see "Sources of Information on *Heliconia*" and "Taxonomic Notes"). The cultivar names have been supplied by gardeners, commercial growers, and collectors. In general, the most commonly used cultivar name has been selected. In an effort to standardize the bewildering array of names currently being applied to heliconias, we encourage readers to adopt the cultivar names selected in this guide. The section "Taxonomic Notes" explains the origin and/or source of the botanical and cultivar names.

The descriptions of the plants are based on our firsthand observations of living plants growing in their native habitats or cultivated in gardens, nurseries, or greenhouses. All of the forms described here have been seen, studied, and collected by one or both of the authors. In most cases, the photographs have been taken by the authors; for several taxa friends and colleagues have graciously supplied photos. In devising and choosing appropriate terminology to describe the plants, we have tried to synthesize, standardize, and simplify where possible. The terms we have used here are appropriate for both scientists and lay persons.

For readers interested in more than just the identification of plants, general background information on the botany and horticulture of heliconias is included in the text and appendices. This information has been presented in a nontechnical fashion comprehensible to the lay person. A glossary of terms is found near the end of the guide. Basic information is provided on the structure of heliconias, where they grow, and how they are pollinated, as well as what defines a species or cultivar of *Heliconia* and how they get their names. A brief section on the botanical relatives of *Heliconia* is also included. For those wishing more information, a list of botanical and horticultural references is provided in "Sources of Information on *Heliconia*."

Information and instructions on the horticulture of *Heliconia* have been made available in several recent publications (see "Sources of Information on *Heliconia*"). However, it is obvious that the art of growing and using heliconias as ornamentals is still in its initial stages of development. For this reason, we invited brief contributions by three horticulturists on the subjects of the cultivation of heliconias (Appendix I), their use in the landscape and interiorscape (Appendix II), and the commercial production of heliconias as cut flowers and potted plants (Appendix III). These sections constitute three points of view on the horticultural aspects of *Heliconia*. We hope that they will serve as an inspiration to readers interested in growing and cultivating these plants.

# Acknowledgments

We are grateful to many people for their help and input in our studies of *Heliconia* and in assembling this guide. We each learned many things from many of the same but also many different people.

For Fred Berry:

Harvey R. Bullis, Jr., got me started on *Heliconia* and gave me the chance. John M. Hall III shared his deep knowledge of botany, ecology, and Costa Rica and was there through the formative phases of the guide; he has my devotion for his dedication and sharing. Bob Wilson gave early stimulation and Iris Bannochie followed through with more. Al Will and Gil Daniels helped through HSI. Lester Pancoast has been one of those special colleagues who shared some great traveling and collecting experiences, as did Jack Dammann, Alan Carle, and Charlie Ullman, who also kept my interest peaking at home.

David Carli made available the super holdings at his fabulous farm, Costa Flores, in Costa Rica, and joined me in starting to understand the heliconias of the Windward Islands and northern South America.

Ray Baker shared his fine knowledge and extensive notes, and led me through the wondrous holdings of Manoa Valley's Lyon Arboretum. In cooperation with Bob Hirano, important research is being carried out with this most diversified collection.

Hamilton Manley really helped at Sunshine Farms as we tiptoed through the psittacorums; thanks also to Rosak Bisel, Rhemigio Dumayag, and Jill LaVine.

Roberto Burle-Marx made his extensive gardens just outside Rio de Janeiro available to study and provided some gems of plant wisdom.

José Abalo opened his collection of heliconias for use and gave Harvey Bullis and me some salient lessons on speciation and ecology.

With special feeling and joy, I thank Cristina Lindley for giving me encouragement, support, and balance, and for being one of the early reasons for pursuing this effort to its completion!

In my travels, collecting, photographing, note-taking, and working in Central and South America, the West Indies, and the United States, many wonderful people helped and shared. In Mexico, Victor Gonzalez and Rene Marquez; in Belize, Winston Miller and Henry Jordan; in Guatemala, Fernando and Nidia Rosales; in Honduras, John Dixon, David Tag, Gustavo Cruz, Enoc Burgos, Mario Espinal, and Sherry Thorne; in Costa Rica, Gary Stiles, Luis Diego Gomez, Chester Skotak, Ronny Williams, Jim Lewis, Eduardo Herrera, and Arlene Benham; in Panama, Argelis Ruiz Guevara; in Colombia, Rod Mast; in Venezuela, Glenda Medina and Paul Berry; in Suriname, Henri and Judy Reichart; and in Brazil, Peter Bacon, Dimitri Sucre, Gilberto de Freitas, Luiz Carlos Gurken, and Eduardo Couto Dalcin. In Trinidad, Hugh Woods, Jake Kenney, and Sandra Barnes; in Grenada, John Criswick and James Findley; in Barbados, John Bannochie and Julia Horrocks; in St. Vincent, Kerwin Morris; in St. Lucia, Horrace Walters; in Dominica, Nigel Lawrence and Terry Robinson; in Puerto Rico, Bob Lankford, Luis and Lilian Rico, and Kelley Brooks; and in the Dominican Republic, Jose Ottenwalder and Patric Vez. In Hawaii, Elsie Horikawa, Roger and Judy Peckenpaugh, Mark Collins, Howard Cooper, Rich Criley, John Duey, John Morgan, Charlotte Yemane, Lillian Oliveira,

Bill Garnet, Dan Lutkenhouse, Ed Johnson, Terry Takiue, Ken and Lisa Vinzant, and Mrs. Moyers; in Florida, Charlie Ullman, Joseph Fondeur, Dexter Ball, Tim Broschat, Henry Donselman, Monroe Birdsey, Trish Frank, Dewey Fisk, Benny Tjia, Robin Wyss, Mark Wilson, David Bar-Zvi, Georgia Tasker, Al Will, David Leicht, Don Evans, Pete Harry, Mark Frederick, Ernesto Alvarez, Peter Pritchard, Ted Sack, Bob Work, Harry Luther, DeArmond Hull, Ernie Lee, Candy Loesner, Judy Hicklin, and Patricia Berry, also Bill Wison and Bob Smith; and in Australia, Alan and Suzi Carle.

Finally and foremost, I thank Alicia Berry and Darrell Berry.

For John Kress:

I would like to thank José Abalo, Lennart Andersson, Ray Baker, Dexter Ball, Tim Broschat, Alan Carle, David Carli, Alii Chang, Lindsay Clarkson, Howard Cooper, Richard Criley, Gil Daniels, Geoff Dennis, Henry Donselman, Tunty Echeverry, Luiz Emygdio de Mello Filho, Joseph Fondeur, Peter Green, Harry Luther, Hamilton Manley, Rob Montgomery, Gustavo Morales, Lester Pancoast, Tim Plowman, Boyo Ramsaroop, Cheryl Roesel, F. Gary Stiles, Dimitri Sucre, Greg and Masako Westcott, Robert Wilson, Keith Woolliams, and countless others around the world who have helped me discover and understand the botany and horticulture of *Heliconia*. I am particularly indebted to all the members of the Heliconia Society International for their enthusiasm about these plants.

I am very grateful for the assistance that the National Science Foundation (Grants DEB-7701556, DEB-7724612, BSR-8306939, BSR-8317553, and BSR-8706524) and the National Geographic Society (Grants 2552-82, 3650-87, 3925-88) have provided me throughout my investigations of the botany of *Heliconia*.

We would especially like to thank Gil Daniels, Joseph Fondeur, Lester Pancoast, Rich Criley, Peter Cannell, John Farrand, and Linda McKnight, who all greatly helped in the production of this book. We both appreciate the financial award from the Regents' Publication Program of the Smithsonian Institution which made the publication of this book possible.

# Description of Plant Features and Morphology

In different technical and popular publications about *Heliconia*, various terms have been used for the same plant structures and features. The descriptions and terms provided here have been chosen to be best suited to the diversity of lay and professional readers of this guide. A glossary is provided near the end for additional clarification of terms.

Heliconias are medium to large erect herbs often with extensive rhizomatous growth (Fig. 1). The patterns of production of rhizomes, branches, and erect shoots result in varying capacities for vegetative colonization. Each erect shoot is composed of a stem and leaves (Fig. 1), and it is often, although not always, terminated by an inflorescence. The stem is made up of an axis covered by overlapping sheathing leaf bases (hence technically called a pseudostem) and can be up to several meters in length. In some species (e.g., *Heliconia platystachys*), the pseudostem has a distinctive white, waxy coat (also sometimes found on inflorescences and the backs of leaf blades).

On the stem the leaves are oppositely arranged in a flat, two-dimensional plane (distichous). Each leaf is composed of a petiole (stalk) and a blade (Fig. 1). Three basic types of leaf arrangements are found in *Heliconia* (Fig. 2); these are normally constant within a species. If the leaves are oriented ver-

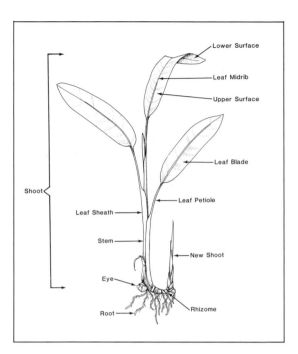

Figure 1. Shoot characters of a heliconia.

tically and have long petioles, the plants have the growth habit
of a banana plant and are called "musoid." If the leaves are
more or less horizontally positioned and the blades have short
petioles, the plants have the aspect of a ginger plant and are
called "zingiberoid." Some species have short or medium-
length petioles with blades that are held obliquely and have a
shoot organization resembling that in species of *Canna;* such
plants are called "cannoid." It should be noted that although
most species will fit into one of these three growth habits,
some plants may be intermediate between basic forms.

The leaf blades are usually green, but in some species
(e.g., *Heliconia reticulata, H. ramonensis, H. imbricata*) they are
often tinted maroon or red below, especially along the mar-

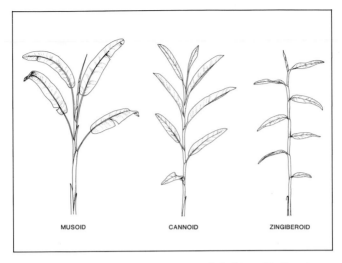

Figure 2. The three basic shoot growth habits of heliconias.

gins. In some species the blades split or become lacerated into narrow lateral segments with age (e.g., *H. chartacea*), or have a thick, white, waxy coat below (e.g., *H. curtispatha, H. collinsiana*). The blade apex is usually pointed and the base is nearly always unequal, with one side extending farther along the petiole.

The most conspicuous feature of a flowering plant is the colorful inflorescence (Fig. 3). Inflorescences are almost always terminal on erect, leafy shoots, but in a few species (e.g., *Heliconia metallica, H. hirsuta*) they may arise on a leafless basal shoot. The inflorescence has either an erect or pendent orientation with respect to the leafy shoot from which it emerges (Fig. 3). The inflorescence is made up of the peduncle (the part of the stem between the terminal leaf sheath and the basal bract), modified leaflike structures called inflorescence bracts (also known as cincinnal bracts, branch bracts, or spathes), the rachis connecting adjacent bracts, and a coil of flowers within each bract (Fig. 3). The rachis may differ from the bracts in

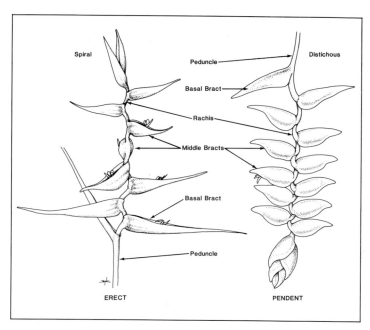

Figure 3. Inflorescence characters of heliconias.

color and texture and is either straight or zigzag. The bracts are in one plane (distichous) or are spirally arranged due to twisting of the rachis. In some species, the rachis is only slightly twisted, making the bracts semispirally arranged (e.g., *H. xanthovillosa*), or are distichous when young, but become spiral as all the bracts mature. The bract closest to the peduncle may be elongated and leaflike.

Once a plant is mature, each shoot that is produced from the rhizome has the potential to generate a single inflorescence. The inflorescence may last from several days to several months on the shoot from which it emerged. Eventually the inflorescence will cease to produce flowers and fruits, turn brown, and dry up or rot away. From that stage the entire shoot will also die as new shoots begin to grow from the underground rhizomes (Fig. 1).

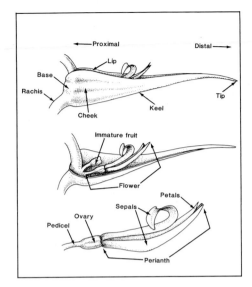

Figure 4. Inflorescence bract and flower
characters of heliconias.

The inflorescence bracts are usually bright red, yellow, or
both, but they are sometimes green (e.g., *H. solomonensis*) or
even pink (e.g., *H. chartacea*). In some species (e.g., *H. psittacorum, H. latispatha*) the bracts are smooth, while in others the
entire inflorescence may be covered by short (e.g., *H. orthotricha*) or long, woolly (e.g., *H. magnifica, H. xanthovillosa*) hairs.

Each inflorescence bract (Fig. 4) contains a varying number of flowers, up to 50 depending on the species. Each flower
in turn is subtended by a small floral bract (removed in Fig. 4).
The floral bracts of some species are opaque and leathery, and
persist through fruit development to protect maturing ovaries.
In other species they are filmy or translucent and quickly de-
compose after the flowers close.

The flowers are hermaphroditic, possessing both male
and female sexual parts. The perianth is made up of three
outer sepals and three inner petals united at the base and to
each other in various ways (Fig. 4). Because the outer envelope

of sepals is the most conspicuous part of the perianth, important features of the sepals are given in the individual descriptions of the species and cultivars. When the flower opens, a single sepal becomes free from the other perianth parts and allows pollinators to enter the flower. The color of the perianth is species specific. The sepals and petals are usually yellow, varying from pale yellow to white at the base and from pale yellow to deep yellow distally. In some species the flowers are green (e.g., *Heliconia latispatha*), or pinkish red (e.g., *H. mariae, H. metallica*), or made up of several colors (e.g., *H. hirsuta*). The sepals can be smooth (e.g., *H. latispatha*) or hairy (e.g., *H. pogonantha*). The flowers are open for only a single day, after which the perianth falls from the ovary.

The flower contains five fertile stamens that produce viable pollen. A sixth stamen is replaced by a sterile staminode that does not produce pollen but may function in some species as a guide leading the pollinator's tongue to the floral nectaries situated at the base of the style.

The ovary lies below the sepals and petals (Fig. 4), and can be variously colored. It is usually smooth in most species but is hairy in others (e.g., *Heliconia trichocarpa*). The pedicel, which attaches the flower in the bract, is usually short and obscured by the floral bracts.

The mature fruit of *Heliconia* is like a peach, a drupe, with a hard inner layer enclosing each of the true seeds (one to three per fruit). The outer layer of the fruit is fleshy, and at maturity the surface layer becomes blue in American species or red to orange in South Pacific species. The colorful fruits are very attractive to the birds and mammals that disperse the seeds.

# Habitats and Geographic Distribution

Heliconias are native primarily to the American tropics, from the Tropic of Cancer in Central Mexico to the Tropic of Capricorn in South America, including the Caribbean. Most species inhabit moist or wet regions, but some are found in seasonally dry areas (Fig. 5). Although heliconias attain their most luxuriant vegetative growth in the humid lowland tropics (Fig. 6) at elevations below 1,500 feet, the greatest numbers of species (many locally endemic) are found in middle-elevation rain and cloud forest habitats (Fig. 7). Few species occur above 6,000 feet.

The most conspicuous members of the genus inhabit open sites in secondary growth along roadsides, on riverbanks, and in patches of light in the forest (Fig. 8). With increased destruction by man of the tropical rain forest, these species readily invade and colonize the newly opened areas. Other species never attain such extensive growth and are restricted to the more shaded habitats of the primary forest. These latter species are often locally endemic and are fast becoming extinct as destruction of the tropical forest accelerates.

A curious disjunct group of heliconias, separated by thousands of miles from most other species, is found in the Old

# COMMON HABITATS OF HELICONIAS

Figure 5. *Heliconia osaënsis* growing in open areas in seasonally dry regions of Costa Rica.

Figure 6. Looking out over the lowland tropical rain forests of Chocó, Colombia. *Heliconia rhodantha* is in the foreground.

Figure 7. The understory of a middle elevation cloud forest in central Panama with *Heliconia longa* and *H. irrasa*.

Figure 8. *Heliconia pogonantha* is abundant in secondary growth of the humid lowlands of Costa Rica.

World tropics. These heliconias are distributed from Samoa in the Pacific Ocean westward to the central Indonesian island of Sulawesi, and all have primarily green bracts and flowers. The means by which these plants reached the South Pacific millions of years ago is still an unanswered question. These species undoubtedly belong in the genus *Heliconia*, even though a separate generic name, *Heliconiopsis*, was once suggested for them. Earlier taxonomists included all of the Old World taxa in a single species, *Heliconia indica*. It is now recognized that six species and several varieties occur naturally in this area. Many of the popular ornamental heliconias with coppery red leaves come from the South Pacific.

As a result of their horticultural and commercial popularity, heliconias are now being grown in nearly all of the tropical regions of the world, including Africa and Asia. In some areas where these species are not native, for example Hawaii and Fiji, some species have escaped from cultivation and are now naturalized in these exotic habitats. It is too early to tell what the impact on native plants will be as a result of the introduction of these foreign species.

# Breeding and Hybridization

In the American tropics, hummingbirds are the exclusive pollinators of *Heliconia* (Figs. 9, 10). In contrast, nectar-feeding bats (Fig. 11) are the main pollinators of the flowers of Old World species. In neotropical heliconias the birds are attracted by the bright red, pink, orange, and yellow colors of the bracts and flowers. The length and curvature of the flower tube in many cases match the length and curvature of the bill of the pollinating hummingbird. Although each flower is open for only one day, there are usually many flowers per bract and many bracts per inflorescence, so that a single plant may be in flower for a long period of time. As the hummingbirds fly from plant to plant probing the flowers for nectar with their long curved bills, pollen is transferred from flower to flower. In this way natural fertilization is achieved and seeds produced.

Most species of *Heliconia* that have been tested so far are self-compatible; that is, a flower will produce seed following self-pollination. However, in most cases in order for seed to be set a pollinator is required to transfer pollen. This can be done by natural or artificial means. This fact accounts for the instances in which seeds and fruits are produced on heliconias cultivated outside their native habitats where the humming-

## POLLINATORS OF HELICONIAS

Figure 9. The Bronzy Hermit (*Glaucis aenea*), a common humming-bird pollinator of neotropical lowland heliconias, perched on an inflorescence bract of *Heliconia pogonantha*. Note the long, curved bill with pollen at its tip.

Figure 10. A Crowned Woodnymph hummingbird (*Thalurania colombica*) probing the flower of *Heliconia imbricata* with its straight bill.

Figure 11. *Melonyc-teris woodfordi*, a species of nectar-feeding bat, is the primary pollinator of *Heliconia solomonensis* in the Solomon Islands. The flowers of this species are open in the evening and at night.

bird or bat pollinators do not occur. Some insects (e.g., earwigs in Hawaii) and vertebrates (honeyeaters in Australia) are quite agile at transferring pollen within a heliconia flower.

On the other hand, it has been found that cross-fertilization between species is generally unsuccessful because pollen of one species is usually inhibited by the other species. Although some natural hybrids have been found (see below), so far there is no solid evidence that any hybrids of *Heliconia* have been artificially made. The results suggest that, in addition to careful emasculation of flowers before crossing, some mechanical or chemical methods will be needed to enable artificial hybrids to be created.

In light of these findings on barriers preventing fertilization between species, it is not surprising that hybridization is relatively rare in nature. The sparsity of natural hybrids exists in spite of the large number of species that grow together in the same habitats and share the same pollinators. Nonetheless, natural hybrids are known. For example, *Heliconia* cv. Golden Torch, one of the most commonly cultivated heliconias, is a natural hybrid between *H. psittacorum* and *H. spathocircinata* discovered in Guyana. In the Windward Islands of the Caribbean, hybrids between *H. caribaea* and *H. bihai* are also common. Other hybrids between species with pendent and erect inflorescences have been found as well (e.g., *H. secunda* × *H. clinophila*, *H. psittacorum* × *H. marginata*).

When heliconias that do not normally grow together are brought into cultivation in the same garden or nursery, some of the natural barriers to hybridization are removed. In these cases, especially in tropical countries where hummingbirds are present, one may expect to see more hybrids appearing as seedlings in the garden.

# Names and Taxonomy

Over 450 botanical names for species, varieties, and hybrids of *Heliconia* have been proposed. In addition, over 200 cultivar and common names have been used in the commercial trade and popular literature. Despite all of these names (many of which apply to the same plants), we are still unsure of how many different forms of heliconias exist. From our experience we estimate that there are about 200 to 250 species of *Heliconia* and probably at least that many forms or cultivars.

What is the meaning of these different categories of names: *species, variety, form, hybrid, cultivar?* The first one, *species*, is probably the most difficult one to define. Not all botanists share the same definition of a species, because the natural barriers that separate species are still unclear. Understanding the interaction of organisms in their native environments is not a simple task, and it is little wonder that no consensus exists as to what a species is. The earliest concept stated that species do not vary at all in their characteristics, but always fit exactly a certain "type." This concept, called the "typological species," was commonly accepted in the 17th and 18th centuries, before the theory of evolution was formulated. As more information became known about genetics in the

1900s, biologists began to recognize that individuals did vary in many characters within and between populations and that species, being made up of individuals, also varied extensively.

The "biological species" concept, which replaced the typological species concept, states that species are groups of actually or potentially interbreeding populations genetically isolated from other such groups by one or more reproductive isolating mechanisms. Although widely separate populations making up a biological species may vary considerably in certain features, this variation is usually slight between adjacent populations. This is why we can put two apparently different forms of *Heliconia bihai* that have different colors and different shapes into the same species if intermediate populations exist between the two forms (i.e., continuous variation is present between the extremes).

A *species* is therefore a group of organisms organized into one or more populations that are separated from other such groups by reproductive isolation and in most cases by recognizable differences in color and form. A species is the basic unit of biological classification and requires a universally accepted botanical name.

A *variety* (abbreviated var.) is a group of organisms forming one or more populations within a species and showing only moderate differences from other groups in the same species. A variety is often geographically separated from other varieties within a species. Varieties also require botanical names. A *subspecies* (abbreviated ssp.) is similar to a variety.

Occasionally individual plants within a species show some minor variation in color or structure that is not sufficient to warrant recognition of a separate variety. These individuals are usually found scattered through the range of the species and are not geographically isolated. This slight variation can be identified by naming a *forma* (abbreviated f.), which is the lowest category in the hierarchy of botanical classification.

A *hybrid* is a cross between two species and possesses features of both parents. Hybrids can be found in nature (natural hybrids) or artificially created in the garden or laboratory.

A *cultivar* (abbreviated cv.), short for "cultivated variety," is a plant that is maintained in cultivation and possesses distinguishing features that are retained when reproduced. Cultivars may be found in wild populations or be artificially created, but are not the same as botanical varieties or forms. It is not uncommon for species, varieties, and hybrids to be given a cultivar name if that entity is grown in cultivation. However, in contrast to botanical names, cultivars should not be given Latin or Greek names. Instead the name is preceded by cv. or enclosed within single quotes; the first letter of each word is always capitalized.

The natural variation that exists among individuals and populations of *Heliconia* has caused much confusion among hobbyists and commercial growers with respect to these categories. If the range of variation within a species has not been carefully studied, it is difficult to accept that two very different looking plants could be the same species throughout its geographic range. In such a case it is very easy to be a "typologist" and want to give a new species name for every minor difference found between plants (more accurately forms or cultivars). Yet the more we study such species as *H. bihai*, *H. stricta*, and *H. psittacorum* with wide geographic distributions, we are finding that a great amount of variation exists within and between populations of the same species.

With over 500 cultivar and species names for heliconias it is no wonder that much confusion exists over finding the correct names. However, botanists have been confronted for hundreds of years with the same problem of applying correct and consistent names for any type of plant. Communication about the ecology, physiology, and economic uses of plants succeeds because of the development of a universally accepted system for naming plants. This same system must be applied in finding the correct Latin names for species of *Heliconia*, as well as the names of cultivars and trade plants.

In the 1600s and 1700s plants were given long descriptive names (called polynomials) that were very cumbersome and difficult to communicate. In 1753, Carolus Linnaeus, a Swedish scientist, established the convention of providing for each species of plant a unique two-part name (binomial) consisting of the genus name followed by the species name. For example, the 1701 polynomial *Bihai amplissimus foliis, florum vasculis coccineus* was eventually replaced with the familiar *Heliconia bihai*, which is still used today.

The correct names for plants are now determined by a set of rules called the "International Code of Botanical Nomenclature," which was first formulated in 1867 and has been revised and refined in thirteen subsequent editions. (There is also an "International Code of Nomenclature for Cultivated Plants" for figuring out the names of cultivars and hybrids.) The Code helps us with such problems as (1) deciding the correct name for a species that has been given more than one name, and (2) choosing which plant deserves a name if that name has been given to more than one species. For example, a species of *Heliconia* was given the name of *H. angusta* by a Brazilian botanist in 1825. Since that time, nine additional names have been published for the same species. The rule of priority states that the earliest legitimately published name is the one we must accept, so we recognize that species as *H. angusta* and relegate the later nine names to "synonymy."

In another case, the name *Heliconia psittacorum* was applied to at least ten different species after it was first given to a plant from Suriname by the son of Linnaeus in 1781. Because an adequate description accompanied the first publication of that name and because a dried specimen (still available for study today) of the described plant was deposited in a Swedish herbarium at the same time, we can accurately determine which of the 10 species deserves the name *H. psittacorum*.

Many other such nomenclatural puzzles exist among the over 400 names for heliconias that have been published in the last 250 years. Unfortunately it is often a painstaking and time-consuming process to track down the correct names, but at least the Code provides us with a set of rules by which to do it.

Investigations of the taxonomy of *Heliconia* are in many cases not simple. To give a name to any species requires both hunting down the correct name out of many possibilities as well as identifying the species itself. The genus *Heliconia* is a particularly difficult one because the plants are large and fleshy, and require study in their natural environments. This book is in part an attempt to dispel some of the confusion about names of *Heliconia*.

In selecting the botanical and horticultural names for this guide, we have followed the International Codes to the best of our ability. The taxonomy of *Heliconia* is currently in dynamic reorganization and we have chosen botanical names in an effort to maintain stability where possible. Cultivar names enjoying the widest usage are given priority here. We have tried not to favor the names used by any particular commercial grower or in a particular geographic area. We have not included species which are unfamiliar to us or those taxonomically unknown unless they are widely cultivated. In such cases we comment on the taxonomic problems in the section "Taxonomic Notes." It is inevitable that some of our designations will change with time. Nonetheless, we hope that this guide will clear up much of the current confusion and provide some consistency in names of heliconias.

# Botanical Relatives of *Heliconia*

*Heliconia* is the only genus in the plant family Heliconiaceae, which is a member of a larger taxonomic category called the order Zingiberales (earlier called the Scitamineae). In addition to the many cellular features that distinguish the Zingiberales from other plants, there are several very conspicuous characters by which they can be recognized, including (1) large leaves with blades possessing transverse venation and often long petioles, and (2) large, usually colorful, bracteate inflorescences. This order is most closely related to the bromeliads (family Bromeliaceae) and their relatives (superorder Bromeliiflorae).

Most current taxonomists recognize eight separate families in the Zingiberales (Fig. 12): Musaceae (the bananas), Strelitziaceae (the birds-of-paradise), Lowiaceae (no common name), Heliconiaceae (the heliconias), Zingiberaceae (the gingers), Costaceae (costus), Cannaceae (the cannas), and Marantaceae (the prayer plants). Most of the members of these eight families are native to the tropical regions of the earth. Many are cultivated as ornamentals.

Figure 12. Diagrammatic representation of the relationships of heliconias (Heliconiaceae) to their relatives in the order Zingiberales.

## FAMILY MUSACEAE (BANANA FAMILY)

Native species of the two genera of the Musaceae, *Musa* (35 species) and *Ensete* (7 species), are restricted to tropical Africa, eastern Asia, Australia, and the South Pacific. However, both genera have been extensively cultivated and hybridized for thousands of years and are now distributed around the world. The spirally arranged leaves, separate male and female flowers, and pulpy fruits distinguish the members of the Musaceae from other Zingiberales. The commercial importance of bananas has always focused attention on this family, especially the edible hybrids of *Musa* (Fig. 13). In addition, several species of *Musa* (*M. acuminata* [Fig. 14], *M. velutina*, *M. coccinea* [Fig. 15], and *M. ornata*) and *Ensete* (*E. ventricosum;* Fig. 16) are cultivated as ornamentals. The family name commemorates Antonius Musa, physician to the first Roman emperor Octavius Augustus.

Figure 13. Edible banana (*Musa acuminata* Colla × *balbisiana* Colla).

Figure 14, upper left. Variegated banana (*Musa acuminata* cv. Aeae).

Figure 15, upper right. Red banana (*Musa coccinea* Andr.).

Figure 16, lower left. Abyssinian banana (*Ensete ventricosum* (Welw.) E.E. Cheesm.).

## FAMILY STRELITZIACEAE (BIRD-OF-PARADISE FAMILY)

The three genera and seven species of the family, *Strelitzia* (five species; Fig. 17), *Ravenala* (one species; Fig. 18), and *Phenako-spermum* (one species; Fig. 19), are restricted to southern Africa, Madagascar, and South America, respectively. Unique features of the Strelitziaceae are the woody trunk (absent in some members of *Strelitzia*), the birdlike appearance of the inflorescence and flowers, and the woody, capsular fruit. The popular birds-of-paradise (*Strelitzia reginae* [Fig.17] and *Strelitzia nicolai*) and traveler's palm (*Ravenala madagascariensis;* Fig. 18) are commonly grown as landscape and greenhouse ornamentals. *Strelitzia* was named to honor Charlotte Sophia of the family Mecklenburg-Strelitz, the consort of King George III of England and a patron of botany.

Figure 17. Bird-of-paradise (*Strelitzia reginae* Ait.; Strelitziaceae).

Figure 18, left. Traveler's palm (*Ravenala madagascariensis* Sonn.; Strelitziaceae).

Figure 19, right. *Phenakospermum guyannense* (L.C. Rich.) Endl. ex Miq. (Strelitziaceae).

## FAMILY LOWIACEAE (NO COMMON NAME)

The single genus of the family, *Orchidantha*, with five to eight species, is found in Southeast Asia and some Pacific islands. *Orchidantha* has always been considered an unusual member of the Zingiberales and is among the most poorly known taxa in the order in terms of botany and horticulture. The specialized leaf blade with several pairs of longitudinal veins parallel to the distinct midrib, the often subterranean inflorescence, and the elaboration of one petal into a large labellum are among the more distinctive features of the family. Several species, for example *O. maxillarioides* (Fig. 20) and *O. fimbriata*, are cultivated in some botanic gardens. The name *Orchidantha* signifies the orchidlike shape of the flowers.

Figure 20. *Orchidantha maxillarioides* (Ridl.) K. Schum. (Lowiaceae).

## FAMILY HELICONIACEAE (HELICONIA FAMILY)

The single genus *Heliconia* has perhaps 250 species (only 180
have so far been described) that are distributed primarily in
the neotropics. *Heliconia* has been variously associated with the
banana family or the bird-of-paradise family, but is now placed
in its own family, Heliconiaceae. The inverted flowers, the
presence of a single staminode, and the peachlike fruits are
special features of *Heliconia*. Many species, varieties, and cultivars are now being grown as pot plants and for cut flowers.
The name *Heliconia* is derived from Helicon, a mountain in
southern Greece regarded by the ancient Greeks as the home
of the Muses, thus suggesting the relationship between these
plants and the bananas (genus *Musa*).

## FAMILY ZINGIBERACEAE (GINGER FAMILY)

The Zingiberaceae, the largest family in the Zingiberales, consist of approximately 50 genera and 1,000 species. Gingers are found in all tropical regions of the world, but are concentrated in the Old World, especially in Southeast Asia. Because of the ephemeral flowers (often lasting less than one day), taxonomic study of the family is difficult. The fusion of two sterile stamens into a labellum and the occurrence of cells containing essential or ethereal oils are features found in all gingers. Members of several genera, including *Alpinia* (Fig. 21), *Amomum, Curcuma, Etlingera* (Fig. 22), *Globba, Hedychium* (Fig. 23), *Kaempferia,* and *Zingiber* (Fig. 24), are grown as ornamentals or as spices. *Zingiber,* the basis of the family name Zingiberaceae, comes from the Sanskrit word *sringavera* meaning "horn-shaped," in reference to the rhizomes.

Figure 21. Red Ginger (*Alpinia purpurata* (Vieill.) Schum.).

Figure 22, upper left. Red Torch Ginger (*Etlingera elatior* (Jack) R.M. Smith).

Figure 23, upper right. Shampoo Ginger (*Zingiber spectabile* Griff.).

Figure 24, bottom. Epiphytic hedychium (*Hedychium longicornutum* Bak.).

## FAMILY COSTACEAE (COSTUS FAMILY)

The Costaceae, consisting of four genera and about 150 species, are distributed throughout the Asian, African, and American tropics. The largest genus, *Costus* (100 species; Figs. 25, 26), is most diverse in the American tropics, but is also found in Africa, Asia, and northern Australia. *Monocostus* (one species; Fig. 27) and *Dimerocostus* (two species) are restricted to the New World tropics. *Tapeinochilos* (20 species; Fig. 28), the most poorly understood genus in the family, extends through New Guinea, Indonesia, and tropical Australia. The well-developed (sometimes branched) stem, the distinctive staircaselike spirally arranged leaves, and the fusion of five sterile stamens into a petaloid labellum are characters unique to the Costaceae. The Costaceae were at first always classified as a subdivision of the ginger family, but are now accepted by the majority of taxonomists as a separate family. Both *Costus* and *Tapeinochilos* are cultivated as ornamentals for landscape and greenhouse use. The name *Costus* (and hence Costaceae) is an old classical name derived from Arabic.

Figure 25. *Costus barbatus* Susseng.

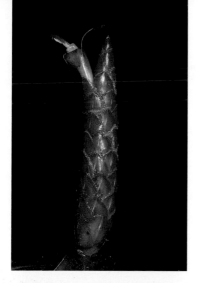

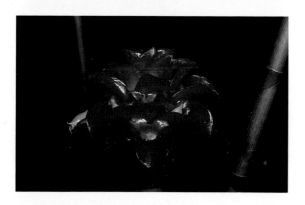

Figure 26, top. *Costus pulverulentus* Presl.

Figure 27, middle. *Monocostus uniflorus* (Poepp. ex Peters.) Maas.

Figure 28, bottom. Indonesian Ginger (*Tapeinochilos ananassae* Hassk.).

## FAMILY CANNACEAE (CANNA FAMILY)

*Canna,* the solitary genus in the family, is primarily found in the New World tropics and subtropics. Estimates on the number of species in *Canna* (Fig. 29) range from nine to 50. The presence of mucilage cells and a petallike style fused to the single fertile stamen are distinctive features of the family. Many hybrid cannas, for example *C.* × *generalis, C.* × *orchioides,* and *C.* × *ehemanii* (Fig. 30), are grown as landscape ornamentals. The name *Canna,* from the Greek *kanna* meaning a reed, most likely refers to the reedlike appearance of the stems.

Figure 29. Indian Shot (*Canna indica* L.).

Figure 30. *Canna* × *ehemanii*.

## FAMILY MARANTACEAE (PRAYER PLANT FAMILY)

The Marantaceae are the second largest family in the order, with 30 genera and 450 to 500 species. Although members of this family are found throughout the tropics, three-quarters of the species, many in the large genus *Calathea* (Figs. 31–33), are found in the neotropics. The classification of the family is still inadequately known. Several special features of the family include the swollen "pulvinus" between the blade and petiole, the sigmoid lateral veins and evenly spaced cross-veins of the leaf blade, the terminal mirror-image pairs of flowers, and the two inner modified stamens which cause an explosive release of pollen. Many members of the Marantaceae are cultivated as ornamental potted plants, especially in the genera *Maranta* (prayer plants), *Calathea* (Figs. 31–33), *Pleiostachya* (Fig. 34), *Stromanthe*, and *Ctenanthe*. The name of the family commemorates Bartolomeo Maranta, an 18th-century Italian botanist.

Figure 31. *Calathea crotalifera* Watson.

Figure 32, upper left. Ice Blue Calathea (*Calathea burle-marxii* H. Kennedy).

Figure 33, upper right. *Calathea lutea* (Aubl.) Schultes.

Figure 34, lower left. *Pleiostachya pruinosa* (Regel) Schum.

# Collecting Heliconias in the Wild

The number of heliconias available for cultivating, decorating, and landscaping is increasing because it is still possible to collect these plants in their natural habitats. Here we give some brief notes on collecting heliconias that include some of our experiences, suggestions, and precautions on bringing them back alive. It is also possible to make valuable dried specimens for study at botanical institutions. However, we limit our comments here to collecting living rhizomes and seeds.

As botanists and horticulturists, one of our greatest satisfactions in life is to search for and find new heliconias in exotic tropical places, to study and record their morphology and growth habits, and to bring back scientific specimens as well as rhizomes and seeds for others to study and enjoy. We've met some wonderful people doing this and have shared some great times with friends on collecting trips. We have also encountered a few serpents and scorpions, a modest number of wasps, howler monkeys, and almost too many angry ants! However, these difficulties are quickly forgotten when an interesting plant is found.

As many of us travel and collect in the tropics, we have become more and more troubled by the rampant destruction of forests and native plants. We rationalize that we are doing a small part to help save some species by collecting and bringing them into cultivation. If we are well informed and conscientious, our efforts certainly can have a direct effect on the survival of these species.

There are a few basic rules that one should follow when collecting plants in other countries. Do not overcollect. It is possible for amateur and commercial collectors to drive a species to extinction. Of course the impact of individual collectors on species extinction is relatively small compared to the consequences of overpopulation and mismanagement of land by large corporations. However, caution is in order. Limit the number of plants collected and do not take more than you can care for. Usually three or four carefully prepared rhizomes are enough to establish the plant in cultivation successfully. Do not collect on private property or in national parks without permission from owners or authorities. Collect only healthy plants and always restore the spot where the plants were collected to as natural condition as possible. If there is a botanical garden in the host country, leave a sample of every specimen you collect for cultivation there. Sometimes one is *required* to leave a set of specimens in the host country (see below under permits). Alternatively, you may leave material in a local private collection. This makes for good public relations and increases the probability of survival of rare species that may suffer during transport back to your country. Also remember to share some of your collected heliconias with one or more of the Heliconia Society International Plant Conservation Centers (see section on HSI).

COLLECTING PERMITS:

Always obtain the necessary plant collecting and export permits required by the local government of the country you are visiting. Often these can be obtained in advance by writing to the Ministry of Agriculture of the host country. Native plants and animals are considered important natural resources in most countries and the authorities can be quite strict with "poachers" who collect and export plant material without proper permits. As mentioned above, in some countries, one must agree to leave a sample of the species collected in order to obtain a permit.

In order to transport living plants from one country to another, various phytosanitary, export, and import permits are required. If you are returning to the United States, you will be required at U.S. Customs to declare any living plants in your possession. To legally import live plant specimens into the United States you must have an "Import permit for plants and plant products." Instructions on restrictions for importing plants and applications for permits can be obtained from the Plant Protection and Quarantine Programs at the U.S. Department of Agriculture (Permit Unit, Animal and Plant Health Inspection Service, Federal Building, Hyattsville, MD 20782).

COLLECTING DATA:

Recording information about where and when a plant was collected is very important. These data are not only important for your own records, but increase the scientific value of the collection. Often some very interesting plants (even new species!) are found by amateur collectors, but without data on locality (usually country, state, province, and town are sufficient), the specimens are of little botanical value. Also, notes on habitat and elevation are important.

COLLECTING EQUIPMENT AND SUPPLIES:

We prefer a short-handled spade (44 inches total) with a sharp, rounded blade (5½ by 16 inches) for digging rhizomes or small clumps (a favorite is one that breaks down into two pieces for easy transport in a travel bag); a sharp knife (hawksbill preferred); a machete (can be used for digging and clearing); a rice-cutter with a very sharp, serrated, curved, six-inch blade; strong plastic or burlap bags for carrying plants; and a bucket (five-gallon) and rubber gloves for dipping rhizomes in pesticides. Expendable supplies include labels, tape, permanent marking pens, and bags for identifying and separating different collections; powdered fungicides, insecticides, and bactericides for dipping and soaking rhizomes; and a vegetable strainer, fungicide, and powdered peat for cleaning and packing seeds.

SELECTING AND PROCESSING COLLECTIONS:

There are two primary means by which most collectors transport living plants of heliconias: by seeds and by rhizomes. Seeds offer several advantages, including less bulk and more genetic variability, but are sometimes difficult to germinate. Ripe fruits (usually pure blue in color) should be collected and the pulp removed by abrasion with a wire mesh vegetable strainer. The clean seeds must then be soaked for five minutes in a dilute bleach solution (or other fungicide) before being placed in plastic bags or paper envelopes filled with finely milled, dry peat moss. Seeds may stay viable for up to one month or more while stored in the peat moss, but in general should be planted as soon as possible.

Propagation by rhizomes is the fastest and most reliable method for collecting and generating heliconias. Select healthy and mature plants with developing eyes (new shoots); dig plants out with as little damage to the rhizomes as possible; remove all roots and loose leaf bases down to the rhizome and cut off excess shoots (above 8" on smaller plants and 14" on larger ones); wash off all soil, any fungal mycelia, and any external parasites (e.g., mealybugs or scale insects); discard any plants with borer holes in shoot or rhizome; dip the cleaned rhizomes in a suitable insecticide for five to 20 seconds depending on the size of the plant; repeat with bactericide and fungicide for five to 20 minutes.

Before packing, exercise rigid quality control by examining each rhizome thoroughly. If additional borer holes are found in the rhizome or shoots, cut into the plant to uncover the extent of damage and discard the plant if infestation is severe. Search carefully for external pests, such as thrips or mealybugs; if found, scrape them off and resoak the plants in insecticide. Pack the cleaned rhizomes in damp paper to prevent damage to the rhizome eyes during shipping. Unpack the plants as soon as possible and always within 15 days. If fungus or mold is found on the rhizomes, wash them off and dip in fungicide. Well-treated rhizomes will remain viable for one to five weeks, depending on health, size, and the viability of the particular species. Recent tests suggest that dipping the cut shoots of rhizomes in antitranspirants prolongs storage time.

# Conservation of Heliconias

[This essay is adapted from an article written by John Kress, which appeared in the *Bulletin* of the Heliconia Society International, Vol. 3, No. 3, 1988.]

In 1983 I took a 12-hour flight to the Solomon Islands, an out-of-the-way spot for most travelers that lies in the middle of the South Pacific nine degrees south of the Equator. Many will remember this tiny group of islands as the site of a critical World War II campaign that took place on the central island of Guadalcanal.

Yet I was heading there in search of something unrelated to the battles that had taken place 40 years before. After stops in Hawaii, Samoa, and Fiji, I arrived in the capital city of Honiara, which then boasted two hotels, three restaurants, and a Japanese War Memorial. In Honiara I met Mr. Geoff Dennis, a knowledgeable plantsman and good friend. He helped me get booked on a small plane to fly across the island where I landed in the soccer field of a tiny village called Mbambanakira. There I met my guide, Kekevera, who led me on a three-mile hike across several rivers to a small village at the base of the mountains.

Upon arrival at the village an hour of sunlight remained. I

Figure 35. Collecting *Heliconia lanata* on Guadalcanal in the
Solomon Islands.

couldn't wait, so we headed up nearby Boghotou Creek into
the hills. It wasn't necessary to go more than a mile before I
saw what I was searching for. Arching out over the water,
rooted in the soil of a steep bank, was a bananalike plant
almost 20 feet tall with large broad leaves and a dangling,
pendent cascade of pure green flowers (Fig. 35). I was only the
third botanist to have ever seen this plant, *Heliconia lanata*, in
the wild. As the sun set, I unsheathed my machete and with
two quick blows the inflorescences, destined to become botanical research specimens, fell into the waiting arms of Kekevera.

As we stumbled back down the ravine, I thought of the
time I first learned that *Heliconia lanata* existed. The evidence
was a dried botanical specimen in the collection at the Royal
Botanic Gardens at Kew, outside London. The specimen had
been collected in the 1960s by an Australian forester as part of
a Royal Society expedition to the Solomon Islands. And here I
was. After a great deal of effort and travel, I had once again
tracked it down in this remote spot in the South Pacific.

I spent the next four days exploring the forests around the

village, making notes, taking photographs, collecting seeds, and preparing preserved specimens of plants which I would carry back to my laboratory for more careful scientific study. *Heliconia lanata* was abundant in the area and the few botanical specimens we collected had little effect on the ecology of the species. My investigations of the classification of heliconias and other tropical plants have taken me around the world several times. The rediscovery of this species fitted another piece to the puzzle of the evolution and origin of these plants.

But why expend the effort and considerable money to find and collect these plants? The reason can best be explained by putting this single species into perspective with the rest of the plants in the world. Biologists estimate that about four and one-half million species of plants and animals exist on the face of the earth. This number includes organisms that live on the land, in the water, and in the air. Two-thirds of them, about three million species, inhabit the tropical areas of the globe. Although we know much about the organisms in the temperate zones, we have named and classified less than one-sixth of the tropical species. In other words, much work remains before we can claim even a satisfactory knowledge of the plants and animals that live with us on this planet.

Modern civilization is heavily dependent on plants and plant products for foods, medicines, building materials, and aesthetic needs. The oxygen we breath is a product of the plants that live on the earth. And tropical plants are the main source of many of the everyday products we use. But how can we expect to utilize tropical plants in the development of new pharmaceuticals and improved crops if we have not even named and described them, or even know of their existence? Tropical forests still contain an untold number of plants that have the potential to greatly increase the standard of living of everyone on earth.

But time is short. It is now quite clear that the tropical forests of the world are being cut down or converted to unusable land at an exceedingly fast rate (Fig. 36). The causes of this massive deforestation in the tropics are many and complex, but

Figure 36. Tropical forest destruction by "slash-and-burn" methods in Panama.

can be basically attributed to overpopulation, economic exploitation, and irresponsibility. Although tropical forests currently cover over more than 15 million square miles of land, nearly 20 thousand square miles are being deforested each year. At this rate all tropical forests, except for a few in biological reserves, will be cut down by the year 2050.

Such large-scale deforestation means massive extinction of the plants and animals that inhabit these forests. For each hour that this rampant cutting of the forests continues, at least one species of tropical plant and one species of animal become extinct. At this rate nearly 20 percent of the earth's plant and animal species will be extinct by the year 2000. The fossil record tells us that this will be the largest mass extinction of living things since the dinosaurs died out nearly 65 million years ago. And it will be caused by the human race.

So there is a reason why a handful of biologists are diligently working in the tropics. Even if we can collect and classify only one-tenth of the tropical plants that remain to be discovered before they become extinct, we will have provided some record of this biological diversity for the appreciation and education of future generations. And for the same reason, plant societies, such as the Heliconia Society International, have the responsibility to get as many species into cultivation as possible to preserve them from extinction.

I recently learned that several Japanese lumber companies have bought up a good portion of the forests in the Solomon Islands and are clear-cutting them for the production of pulp-wood. The rain forests around the village of Mbambanakira, which once seemed like a remote spot, are now also in danger of total destruction. Fortunately, at least the plants I collected in 1983 are thriving in the Plant Conservation Centers sponsored by the Heliconia Society International. The other species inhabiting Boghotou Creek above the village will undoubtedly have a different fate.

# The Heliconia Society International

The excitement generated over the "discovery" of heliconias by horticulturists, gardeners, nurserymen, and florists led to the formation in 1985 of a new plant society dedicated to these tropical ornamentals. The Heliconia Society International (HSI) was established "to increase the enjoyment and understanding of *Heliconia* and related plants through education, research, and communication." Since its beginning, the Society has grown to include members from many states and countries representing a diversity of backgrounds and specialties. Through the publication of the quarterly *Bulletin* and the Annual Meetings information on the cultivation and botany of heliconias is centralized and distributed to members. To promote conservation, HSI has established six Plant Conservation Centers (Andromeda Gardens, Flamingo Gardens, Harold L. Lyon Arboretum, National Tropical Botanical Garden, Jardín Botánico Robert y Catherine Wilson, and Jurong BirdPark; see "Where to See Heliconias"). These centers are establishing germplasm banks of heliconias and relatives, thereby ensuring *ex situ* conservation. Readers interested in joining the Society or in obtaining copies of the *Bulletin* should write to the Heliconia Society International Headquarters, c/o Flamingo Gardens, 3750 Flamingo Road, Ft. Lauderdale, Florida 33330, U.S.A.

# How to Use This Guide

Readers unfamiliar with the basic structures and features of heliconia plants should review the material presented in the section "Description of Plant Features and Morphology." Names and terms for plant parts and growth forms are simply defined and line drawings clearly illustrate important features. These pages supply all the information necessary for understanding the species and cultivar descriptions (also consult the Glossary).

The photographs included in the guide were selected to aid in identification and to give an overall impression of the particular species or cultivar described. A few heliconias are identifiable by their foliage, but most species and cultivars require an inflorescence for accurate identification. In an effort to minimize confusing terminology, no written keys have been provided. To identify a species or cultivar of *Heliconia*, one need only flip through the pages of the center section, making direct comparisons of the color photographs with the plant under consideration. Some confusion may arise when the inflorescence in hand is either very old or very young, or is lacking some essential identifying feature such as mature flowers or seeds. However, these cases should be few.

Each of the 200 heliconias is presented on a separate page

in a standard format, including a color photograph of the inflorescence and brief notes on the following:

(1) Key Inflorescence Characters: in order to simplify identification, the species and cultivars are grouped by inflorescence habits, e.g., erect vs. pendent, distichous vs. spiral;

(2) Name: species, varieties (var.), subspecies (ssp.), cultivars (cv.), and hybrids ($\times$);

(3) Blooming: range of months in which the form is known or predicted to be in flower, including both native and cultivated habitats. This information generally applies to the Northern Hemisphere. Note that a form may bloom all year in its native habitat, but only a limited number of months in cultivation;

(4) Height: the estimated range in feet for overall height of mature plants; in old clumps or plants grown under extraordinary conditions heights may fall outside this range;

(5) Habitat: the general range in percent shade during an average day or season in which mature plants can be expected to grow (without other limiting factors);

(6) Distribution: given first is the native distribution where the form originated, is known to grow, or is expected to be found; the origin of some cultivars is listed as "uncertain"; given second in brackets are the important states and/or countries where the forms are currently cultivated;

(7) Inflorescence: diagnostic colors of major parts of inflorescences and flowers are described; other critical features (e.g., fruit colors) are provided when necessary;

(8) Vegetation: growth habits (musoid, cannoid, zingiberoid) and diagnostic features of the leaves and pseudostems are given when useful in identification.

The 200 forms of *Heliconia* depicted here are organized in broad categories by inflorescence features listed along the edge of each page (erect vs. pendent; distichous vs. spirally arranged). Within these broad categories, the species and cultivars are grouped according to shoot habit (musoid, cannoid, zingiberoid) and inflorescence bract shape (broad vs. narrow). This arrangement will aid readers in identifying species by clustering similar forms together. Within a species, cultivars are organized in alphabetical order. To identify a form, one need only to ascertain if the inflorescence is erect or pendent, distichous or spirally arranged, and then locate the pertinent plants by the sections marked with the Key Inflorescence Characters.

If a species or cultivar name is known to the reader, but not the diagnostic features of the plant, the "Index of Taxa," which alphabetically lists all names of *Heliconia* (botanical and horticultural) included in the guide, can be consulted. The appropriate page representing the form can then be located and studied.

It must be remembered that less than one-half of all forms of *Heliconia* are contained in this guide. Many heliconias found in the wild as well as recent introductions into horticulture will not appear in these pages. In those cases one can compare the plant with the forms included in the guide and temporarily label it with the name of the form it most closely resembles, e.g., *Heliconia* aff. *latispatha* cv. Orange Gyro ("aff." meaning *affinis* or akin to). For proper identification it is best to consult a taxonomic specialist. It is also advisable to periodically check the *Bulletin* of the Heliconia Society International, where new forms are continually illustrated and described.

The authors know from experience that there remain many undescribed species in the wild, as well as many un-identified forms yet to be brought into cultivation. This guide is therefore only a beginning.

*Heliconia caribaea* Lamarck cv. Barbados Flat

BLOOMING.   All year with peak April to October

HEIGHT.   12 to 18 feet

HABITAT.   Full sun to 30% shade

DISTRIBUTION.   St. Lucia [Florida, Hawaii, Barbados, Costa Rica]

INFLORESCENCE.

*Bracts.*  8 to 10; red over most of bract with yellow proximal lip and narrow strip at base, changing to clear lip and green at tip; basal bract mostly green; bracts laterally flattened (not expanded)

*Rachis.*  Red with white at basal bracts

*Sepals.*  White basally to green distally with dark green stripe

*Ovary.*  White

*Pedicel.*  White

VEGETATION.   Musoid; white waxy coating on shoot, petiole, and lower leaf surface, and on lower bracts of inflorescence

*Heliconia caribaea* Lamarck cv. Black Magic

BLOOMING.  April to October

HEIGHT.  12 to 16 feet

HABITAT.  Full sun to 50% shade

DISTRIBUTION.  Dominica [Florida, Costa Rica]

INFLORESCENCE.

*Bracts.*  10 to 14; dark burgundy over most of bract, red at base, green on distal lip and at tip

*Rachis.*  Red

*Sepals.*  White basally to green distally

*Ovary.*  White

*Pedicel.*  White

VEGETATION.  Musoid; white waxy coating on shoot, petiole, and lower leaf surface

*Heliconia caribaea* Lamarck cv. Chartreuse

BLOOMING.    February to November

HEIGHT.    12 to 18 feet

HABITAT.    Full sun to 40% shade

DISTRIBUTION.    West Indies [Florida, Hawaii, Brazil]

INFLORESCENCE.

*Bracts.* 11 to 12; brilliant yellow-green; yellow at base, on proximal lip, and on upper bracts along proximal keel, green distally; bracts on younger inflorescences nearly all green

*Rachis.* Yellow

*Sepals.* Green distally and white proximally

*Ovary.* White

*Pedicel.* White

VEGETATION.    Musoid; white waxy coating on stem, petiole, and lower surface of leaf blade

*Heliconia caribaea* Lamarck cv. Cream

BLOOMING.    April to December

HEIGHT.    12 to 16 feet

HABITAT.    Full sun to 40% shade

DISTRIBUTION.    West Indies [Florida, Hawaii]

INFLORESCENCE.

*Bracts.* 10 to 22; gold over most of base and proximal lip, shading to yellow on proximal cheek and cream to green tint on distal cheek to cream-green on keel; indistinct red area on mid-lip and red or pink splotches on cheek (the red-pink increasing with age)

*Rachis.* Pale yellow

*Sepals.* Green distally and white below

*Ovary.* White

*Pedicel.* White

VEGETATION.    Musoid; dense white waxy coating on stem, petiole, and lower surface of leaf blade

*Heliconia caribaea* Lamarck cv. Flash

BLOOMING.    April to December

HEIGHT.    13 to 15 feet

HABITAT.    Full sun to 40% shade

DISTRIBUTION.    Windward Caribbean Islands [Florida, Hawaii]

INFLORESCENCE.

*Bracts.* 8 to 10; red to pink over proximal cheek and keel, yellow at base and on proximal lip, green on distal keel, lip and tip, becoming more yellow on upper bracts

*Rachis.* Yellow to pink

*Sepals.* Green distally to white at base

*Ovary.* White

*Pedicel.* White

VEGETATION.    Musoid; white waxy coating on stem, petiole, and lower surface of leaf blade

*Heliconia caribaea* Lamarck cv. Gold

BLOOMING.   August to December

HEIGHT.   12 to 14 feet

HABITAT.   Full sun to 40% shade

DISTRIBUTION.   West Indies [Florida, Hawaii]

INFLORESCENCE.

*Bracts.* 6 to 10; gold over most of bract, some shading to yellow on keel; green on distal keel, lip, and tip (decreasing on upper bracts); younger bracts may have small amounts of pink or red splashes, but bracts gold when mature

*Rachis.* Gold shading to yellow and yellow-white

*Sepals.* Green on distal third to white below

*Ovary.* White

*Pedicel.* White

VEGETATION.   Musoid; white waxy coating on stem, petiole, and lower surface of leaf blade

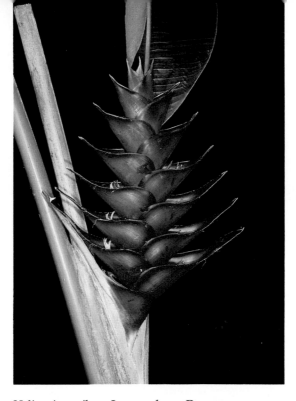

*Heliconia caribaea* Lamarck cv. Purpurea

BLOOMING.   February to November

HEIGHT.   7 to 20 feet

HABITAT.   Full sun to 60% shade

DISTRIBUTION.   West Indies [Florida, Hawaii, Costa Rica]

INFLORESCENCE.

*Bracts.* 5 to 22; red; the upper young bracts sometimes with yellow or green distal lips

*Rachis.* Red

*Sepals.* Green stripes and greenish tint on distal third and white below, some with small yellow area at the base

*Ovary.* White or cream

*Pedicel.* White or cream-yellow

VEGETATION.   Musoid; white waxy coating on most stems, petioles, and lower leaf surfaces

*Heliconia caribaea* Lamarck × *H. bihai* (L.) L.
cv. Carib Flame

BLOOMING. June to
August

HEIGHT. 8 to 15 feet

HABITAT. Full sun to 30%
shade

DISTRIBUTION. Grenada
[Florida]

INFLORESCENCE.

*Bracts.* 7 to 9; red over most
of bract with orange infusion on mid-cheek and thin
yellow-green lip; basal bract
almost all green and second
bract with green keel

*Rachis.* Green below and
red above on lower 3 bracts,
upper bracts with yellow
below and red above

*Sepuls.* Green distally and
white below

*Ovary.* White

*Pedicel.* White

VEGETATION. Musoid

*Heliconia caribaea* Lamarck × *H. bihai*
(L.) L. cv. Criswick

BLOOMING.   April
to October

HEIGHT.   8 to 19 feet

HABITAT.   Full sun to 50%
shade

DISTRIBUTION.   Grenada
[Florida, Hawaii, Brazil]

INFLORESCENCE.

*Bracts.*  8 to 16; red with
minute greenish tip and
very thin yellow-green edge
of lip; basal bracts with
green keel

*Rachis.*  Red

*Sepals.*  Green on distal half,
white below

*Ovary.*  White or pale yellow

*Pedicel.*  White

VEGETATION.   Musoid

*Heliconia caribaea* Lamarck × *H. bihai* (L.) L. cv. Grand Etang

BLOOMING.   May to November

HEIGHT.   9 to 15 feet

HABITAT.   Full sun to 40% shade

DISTRIBUTION.   Grenada [Florida, Hawaii, Barbados]

INFLORESCENCE.

*Bracts.* 9 to 14; dark red to maroon, thin clear distal lip, small green tip; basal bract mostly green, pale green keel on second and third bracts

*Rachis.* Red

*Sepals.* Light green on distal third and white proximally

*Ovary.* White

*Pedicel.* White

VEGETATION.   Musoid; some shoots with white waxy coating, extending onto petiole and lower midrib

*Heliconia caribaea* Lamarck × *H. bihai* (L.) L.
cv. Green Thumb

BLOOMING.    April to
November

HEIGHT.    12 to 16 feet

HABITAT.    Full sun to 30%
shade

DISTRIBUTION.    West
Indies [Costa Rica]

INFLORESCENCE.

*Bracts.* 8 to 13; bright red at
base and on proximal lip
with dark maroon on cen-
tral cheek, green on distal
keel, lip, and tip; basal bract
mostly green, sometimes
with waxy coating

*Rachis.* Bright red

*Sepals.* Green on distal half
and white below

*Ovary.* White

*Pedicel.* White

VEGETATION.    Musoid;
white, waxy coating
on stems

*Heliconia caribaea* Lamarck × *H. bihai* (L.) L.
cv. Grenadier

BLOOMING.   June to
August

HEIGHT.   8 to 14 feet

HABITAT.   Full sun to 40%
shade

DISTRIBUTION.   Grenada
[Florida]

INFLORESCENCE.

*Bracts.*  7 to 11; red over
most of bract with thin yellowish lip and small green
tip; basal bract with green
on keel

*Rachis.*  Red

*Sepals.*  Green on distal half
and white below

*Ovary.*  White

*Pedicel.*  White

VEGETATION.   Musoid

*Heliconia caribaea* Lamarck × *H. bihai* (L.) L. cv. Jacquinii

BLOOMING.   May to November

HEIGHT.   6 to 14 feet

HABITAT.   Full sun to 40% shade

DISTRIBUTION.   Grenada [Florida, Hawaii, Puerto Rico, Venezuela]

INFLORESCENCE.

*Bracts.* 4 to 10; red on lower cheek and keel, yellow or gold at base and broadly along lip, tip green; basal bract with green keel [plants vary in degree of imbrication of bracts]

*Rachis.* Yellow or golden

*Sepals.* Green distally and white below

*Ovary.* White

*Pedicel.* White

VEGETATION.   Musoid

*Heliconia caribaea* Lamarck × *H. bihai* (L.) L.
cv. Kawauchi

BLOOMING.   Peak June and July into December

HEIGHT.   12 to 14 feet

HABITAT.   Full sun to 40% shade

DISTRIBUTION.   Uncertain [Hawaii]

INFLORESCENCE.

*Bracts.* 5 to 7; red with narrow gold-yellow lip proximally, extending distally on upper bracts, tip green; basal bract green over most of keel with some white waxy coating

*Rachis.* Red, becoming yellow between upper bracts

*Sepals.* Green on distal half and white below

*Ovary.* White

*Pedicel.* White

VEGETATION.   Musoid; white waxy coating on stem, petiole, and lower midrib

*Heliconia caribaea* Lamarck × *H. bihai* (L.) L.
cv. Richmond Red

BLOOMING. April to
December

HEIGHT. 9 to 15 feet

HABITAT. Full sun to 40%
shade

DISTRIBUTION. St. Vin-
cent [Hawaii, Florida, Barbados, Costa Rica,
Venezuela]

INFLORESCENCE.

*Bracts.* 7 to 17; red over
most of bract with maroon
at base of lower bracts, or all
red or all maroon, narrow
yellow lip (distal on lower
bracts and all along lip on
upper bracts), small green
tip; basal bract with more
green, especially on distal
keel

*Rachis.* Dark red

*Sepals.* Green on distal half
and white below

*Ovary.* Cream-white

*Pedicel.* Cream-white

VEGETATION. Musoid;
white waxy coating on
stem, petiole, and lower
midrib

*Heliconia caribaea* Lamarck × *H. bihai* (L.) L.
cv. Vermillion Lake

BLOOMING.   June to
August

HEIGHT.   9 to 16 feet

HABITAT.   Full sun to 40%
shade

DISTRIBUTION.   Grenada
[Florida]

INFLORESCENCE.

*Bracts.* 5 to 7; red over most
of bract with orange infusion on upper cheek, yellow
lip and tip; light green on
keel of basal bracts

*Rachis.* Red above and
yellowish below

*Sepals.* Green on distal half
and white below

*Ovary.* White

*Pedicel.* White

VEGETATION.   Musoid

*Heliconia caribaea* Lamarck × *H. bihai* (L.) L. cv. Yellow Dolly

BLOOMING. June to August

HEIGHT. 9 to 14 feet

HABITAT. Full sun to 40% shade

DISTRIBUTION. Grenada [Florida]

INFLORESCENCE.

*Bracts.* 7 to 11; red on proxi-mal cheek and keel with yellow on distal keel, cheek, and lip

*Rachis.* Red above and yellow below

*Sepals.* Green distally and white below

*Ovary.* White

*Pedicel.* White

VEGETATION. Musoid

*Heliconia bihai* (L.) L. cv. Arawak

BLOOMING. December to August

HEIGHT. 5 to 20 feet

HABITAT. Full sun to 40% shade

DISTRIBUTION. Dominica to Grenada [Florida, Hawaii, Costa Rica, Venezuela]

INFLORESCENCE.

*Bracts.* 5 to 11; typically red over most of bract with narrow area of yellow or pale orange on upper cheek and lip and often with green on distal lip and tip; basal bract with green along all or distal part of keel; variations of shading to mostly orange or yellow distally

*Rachis.* Dark red, some with orange on upper bracts

*Sepals.* White with green tip

*Ovary.* White

*Pedicel.* White

VEGETATION. Musoid

*Heliconia bihai* (L.) L. cv. Aurea

BLOOMING. November to August, possibly all year

HEIGHT. 10 to 18 feet

HABITAT. Full sun to 30% shade

DISTRIBUTION. Venezuela [Florida, Hawaii, Costa Rica]

INFLORESCENCE.

*Bracts.* 6 to 12; dark red over most of cheek (decreasing on upper bracts), green along lip, distal keel, and tip, yellow on proximal keel and upper cheek (increasing in area on upper bracts), basal bract mostly green; bracts with white waxy coat distally

*Rachis.* Maroon to dark red between lower bracts, changing to red and yellow between upper bracts

*Sepals.* Green distally and white with yellow tint below

*Ovary.* Cream

*Pedicel.* Cream with yellow tint or white

VEGETATION. Musoid

*Heliconia bihai* (L.) L. cv. Balisier

BLOOMING.  All year

HEIGHT.  5 to 12 feet

HABITAT.  Full sun to 50% shade

DISTRIBUTION.  Trinidad and northern South America [Florida, Hawaii, Costa Rica]

INFLORESCENCE.

*Bracts.*  8 to 22; red over most of bract, usually with a narrow green lip, on some with a slight yellow streak beneath green, keel and tip green; bracts swollen laterally at base

*Rachis.*  Dark to light red

*Sepals.*  Dark to light green distally with a dark green tip, white proximally

*Ovary.*  White or cream

*Pedicel.*  White with yellowish tint on some

VEGETATION.  Musoid

*Heliconia bihai* (L.) L. cv. Banana Split

BLOOMING.   About April to November

HEIGHT.   About 5 to 18 feet

HABITAT.   Full sun to 40% shade

DISTRIBUTION.   St. Vincent [Florida, Hawaii, Costa Rica]

INFLORESCENCE.

*Bracts.* 6 to 9; chocolate (= burnt sienna) covering 10 to 80% of upper bracts, lip green distally, less chocolate on lower bracts

*Rachis.* Chocolate to greenish-yellow

*Sepals.* Green distally and white below

*Ovary.* Yellow

*Pedicel.* Yellow

VEGETATION.   Musoid

*Heliconia bihai* (L.) L. cv. Chocolate Dancer

BLOOMING.    April to November

HEIGHT.    6 to 11 feet

HABITAT.    Full sun to 40% shade

DISTRIBUTION.    St. Vincent [Florida, Hawaii, Costa Rica]

INFLORESCENCE.

*Bracts.* 6 to 9; chocolate (= burnt sienna) covering more than 90% of cheek, base, and keel; narrow area along lip with light green stripe above and yellow below with small green tip; basal bract with partial green keel

*Rachis.* Chocolate with small yellow area at medial base

*Sepals.* Green distally and white below

*Ovary.* White with yellow tint

*Pedicel.* White

VEGETATION.    Musoid

*Heliconia bihai* (L.) L. cv. Emerald Forest

BLOOMING.  April to November

HEIGHT.  4 to 12 feet

HABITAT.  Full sun to 40% shade

DISTRIBUTION.  St. Lucia [Florida, Hawaii, Costa Rica]

INFLORESCENCE.

*Bracts.*  6 to 9; green, yellow, and/or white at base of upper bracts

*Rachis.*  Mainly white or white and yellow

*Sepals.*  Primarily white, green median stripes distally

*Ovary.*  White

*Pedicel.*  White

VEGETATION.  Musoid

*Heliconia bihai* (L.) L. cv. Five A.M.

BLOOMING.   June to December

HEIGHT.   12 to 20 feet

HABITAT.   Full sun to 20% shade

DISTRIBUTION.   Uncertain [Costa Rica]

INFLORESCENCE.

*Bracts.* 6 to 9; light to dusky red at base onto proximal cheek and keel, green distally on lip, cheek, and keel, light yellow on proximal lip; basal bract green

*Rachis.* Red to yellowish

*Sepals.* Primarily white, green medially

*Ovary.* White to cream

*Pedicel.* White

VEGETATION.   Musoid

*Heliconia bihai* (L.) L. cv. Giant
Lobster Claw

BLOOMING.   June to March

HEIGHT.   8 to 18 feet

HABITAT.   Full sun to 60% shade

DISTRIBUTION.   Uncertain [Hawaii, Barbados, Brazil]

INFLORESCENCE.

*Bracts.* 8 to 14; dark red over most of cheek (darkest distally), green lip and tip extending onto distal keel, thin yellow stripe beneath proximal green lip, yellow and green area around base onto lower proximal keel; basal bract mostly green; bracts swollen laterally at base

*Rachis.* Green to dark green

*Sepals.* Green distally, white below

*Ovary.* White

*Pedicel.* White

VEGETATION.   Musoid

*Heliconia bihai* (L.) L. cv. Hatchet

BLOOMING. May to August
HEIGHT. 6 to 10 feet
HABITAT. 20 to 40% shade
DISTRIBUTION. St. Vincent [Florida]

INFLORESCENCE.

*Bracts.* 4 to 7; dark red
*Rachis.* Red
*Sepals.* Green distally and white below
*Ovary.* White
*Pedicel.* White

VEGETATION. Musoid

*Heliconia bihai* (L.) L. cv. Jaded Forest

BLOOMING.   June to October

HEIGHT.   3 to 18 feet

HABITAT.   Full sun to 60% shade

DISTRIBUTION.   St. Lucia [Barbados, Costa Rica]

INFLORESCENCE.

*Bracts*.  3 to 10; green
*Rachis*.  Green
*Sepals*.  Primarily white with greenish stripes distally
*Ovary*.  White
*Pedicel*.  White

VEGETATION.   Musoid

*Heliconia bihai* (L.) L. cv. Kamehameha

BLOOMING.   June to November

HEIGHT.   5 to 11 feet

HABITAT.   Full sun to 30% shade

DISTRIBUTION.   Uncertain [Hawaii]

INFLORESCENCE.

*Bracts.*  6; red along cheek and yellow at base, on keel, and on lip, distal lip and tip with some green; basal bract mostly green

*Rachis.*  Mainly yellow

*Sepals.*  Green distally and white below

*Ovary.*  White

*Pedicel.*  White

VEGETATION.   Musoid

*Heliconia bihai* (L.) L. cv. Kuma Negro

BLOOMING.   July

HEIGHT.   12 to 20 feet

HABITAT.   Full sun to 40% shade

DISTRIBUTION.   Guyana [Costa Rica]

INFLORESCENCE.

*Bracts.* 8 to 12; dark red over most of cheek and proximal keel with green on lip and distal keel, yellow at base

*Rachis.* Yellow with some green

*Sepals.* Green distally and white below

*Ovary.* White

*Pedicel.* White

VEGETATION.   Musoid

*very slightly spiral

*Heliconia bihai* (L.) L. cv. Lobster Claw One

BLOOMING.   April to December

HEIGHT.   5 to 16 feet

HABITAT.   Full sun to 30% shade

DISTRIBUTION.   Northern South America [widely cultivated]

INFLORESCENCE.

*Bracts.* 7 to 12; red over most of bract with green tip, lip dark green distally with whitish line above, some-times with thin pale yellow line beneath green lip and on distal keel (especially on upper bracts)

*Rachis.* Red

*Sepals.* Green distally and white below

*Ovary.* White

*Pedicel.* White

VEGETATION.   Musoid; lower midrib with maroon stripe from base to about half, leaves slightly undulate

*Heliconia bihai* (L.) L. cv. Lobster Claw Two

BLOOMING.    All year

HEIGHT.    8 to 14 feet

HABITAT.    Full sun to 30% shade

DISTRIBUTION.    Uncertain [Hawaii, Brazil]

INFLORESCENCE.

*Bracts.* 7 to 13; pinkish at base, red-orange over most of bract (paler on lower cheek), green on distal lip, keel (of lower bracts), and tip, thin yellow stripe under most of green lip, on some extending from lip to base

*Rachis.* Pink

*Sepals.* Green distally and white below

*Ovary.* White

*Pedicel.* White

VEGETATION.    Musoid; stem red

*Heliconia bihai* (L.) L. cv. Nappi

BLOOMING.  April to August

HEIGHT.  8 to 15 feet

HABITAT.  Full sun to 30% shade

DISTRIBUTION.  Guyana [Costa Rica, Brazil, Venezuela]

INFLORESCENCE.

*Bracts.*  8 to 12; pale red to red over most of cheek (except basal bract), green along lip and distal keel; yellow at base, along proximal keel and thinly below green lip proximally

*Rachis.*  Red to yellow with pink or green tint

*Sepals.*  Light to dark green distally and white below

*Ovary.*  White

*Pedicel.*  White

VEGETATION.  Musoid

*slightly spiral

*Heliconia bihai* (L.) L. cv. Nappi Yellow

BLOOMING.    July to March

HEIGHT.    12 to 15 feet

HABITAT.    Full sun to 80% shade

DISTRIBUTION.    Guyana [Hawaii, Brazil, Costa Rica, Venezuela]

INFLORESCENCE.

*Bracts.*  6 to 8; bright red at base and on proximal cheek with yellow over distal bract and along keel (some shaded with green); green along lip, tip, and some on distal keel

*Rachis.*  Bright to dark red

*Sepals.*  Light to dark green distally and white or clear below

*Ovary.*  White, some with yellow tint

*Pedicel.*  White, some with green tint

VEGETATION.    Musoid

*becoming spiral

*Heliconia bihai* (L.) L. cv. Purple Throat

BLOOMING.   July

HEIGHT.   16 to 18 feet

HABITAT.   Full sun to 30% shade

DISTRIBUTION.   Uncertain [Hawaii, Costa Rica]

INFLORESCENCE.

*Bracts.* 7 to 10; bright red over most of bract, shading to dark red distally, green on tip and distal keel (of upper bracts), lip green with yellow tint beneath proximally

*Rachis.* Bright red

*Sepals.* Light to dark green distally and white below

*Ovary.* White

*Pedicel.* White

VEGETATION.   Musoid; petioles deep maroon

*slightly spiral

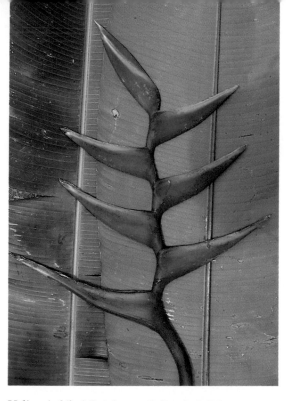

*Heliconia bihai* (L.) L. cv. Schaefer's Bihai

BLOOMING.  All year

HEIGHT.  8 to 12 feet

HABITAT.  20 to 60% shade

DISTRIBUTION.  Venezuela [Florida]

INFLORESCENCE.

*Bracts.* 6 to 10; red over most of bract, green on distal lip and tip, yellow on proximal lip beneath green

*Rachis.* Dark red to red

*Sepals.* Green distally and white proximally

*Ovary.* White

*Pedicel.* White

VEGETATION.  Musoid

*Heliconia stricta* Huber cv. Swish

BLOOMING.  May to November

HEIGHT.  6 to 8 feet

HABITAT.  20 to 40% shade

DISTRIBUTION.  Ecuador [Hawaii]

INFLORESCENCE.

*Bracts.* 5 to 7; red to red-orange over most of bract, green on distal lip, on tip, and on distal keel of lower bracts, yellow along keel proximally; basal bract with green keel

*Rachis.* Yellow with small amount of pink

*Sepals.* Green distally and white below

*Ovary.* White

*Pedicel.* White

VEGETATION.  Musoid; leaves lacerating into broad lateral segments

*Heliconia bihai* (L.) L. cv. Yellow Dancer

BLOOMING.   April to November

HEIGHT.   5 to 14 feet

HABITAT.   Full sun to 50% shade

DISTRIBUTION.   St. Vincent [Florida, Hawaii, Costa Rica]

INFLORESCENCE.

*Bracts.* 5 to 12; yellow on most of bract, green on keel, tip, and lip of lower bracts

*Rachis.* Yellow

*Sepals.* Green and white distally and white below

*Ovary.* Cream-yellow

*Pedicel.* White

VEGETATION.   Musoid

*Heliconia bihai* (L.) L. × *H. spathocircinata*
Aristeg. cv. Cinnamon Twist

BLOOMING.   All year

HEIGHT.   5 to 11 feet

HABITAT.   Full sun to 50% shade

DISTRIBUTION.   Guyana [Florida, Hawaii, Costa Rica]

INFLORESCENCE.

*Bracts.*  5 to 7; red shading to garnet toward tip with yellow and green stripes along lip, or only thin yellow along lip and on tip; basal bract mostly green-yellow

*Rachis.*  Scarlet

*Sepals.*  Greenish yellow distally and white to yellow below

*Ovary.*  White or pale green

*Pedicel.*  Yellow

VEGETATION.   Musoid; lower surface with scarlet midrib and scarlet on stem

*Heliconia wagneriana* Petersen

BLOOMING.   January to September with peak in April to May

HEIGHT.   5 to 15 feet

HABITAT.   Full sun to 40% shade

DISTRIBUTION.   Belize and Guatemala through Central America to Colombia [widely cultivated]

INFLORESCENCE.

*Bracts.* 6 to 20; somewhat variable, bright red area covering most of cheek (pale pink on some), green along lip, keel, and on tip, yellow area at base extending between green lip and keel and red cheek

*Rachis.* Cream or white, some with yellow or green tint

*Sepals.* Dark green distally, white or clear below

*Ovary.* White

*Pedicel.* White

VEGETATION.   Musoid; upper leaf blade usually with maroon midrib, blades undulate

*Heliconia rodriguensis* Aristeguieta

BLOOMING.   September

HEIGHT.   6 to 13 feet

HABITAT.   Full sun to 30% shade

DISTRIBUTION.   Venezuela [Florida]

INFLORESCENCE.

*Bracts.*  10 to 12; deep red to red over most of bract with green lip, tip, and distal keel

*Rachis.*  Pink to red

*Sepals.*  Light green to green distally, white proximally

*Ovary.*  White

*Pedicel.*  White

VEGETATION.   Musoid

*Heliconia stricta* Huber cv. Bob Wilson

BLOOMING.    July to January, possibly all year

HEIGHT.    4 to 8 feet

HABITAT.    Full sun to 40% shade

DISTRIBUTION.    Uncertain [Brazil, Costa Rica]

INFLORESCENCE.

*Bracts.* Red over most of bract, green along distal lip, some yellow along keel

*Rachis.* Red

*Sepals.* Dark green distally with green-white tip, white proximally

*Ovary.* White

*Pedicel.* White

VEGETATION.    Musoid; leaves with undulating margins, usually with maroon midrib on upper and lower surfaces when young and fading with age

*Heliconia stricta* Huber cv. Bucky

BLOOMING.  September to March

HEIGHT.  4 to 7 feet

HABITAT.  20 to 50% shade

DISTRIBUTION.  Guyana [Florida, Costa Rica]

INFLORESCENCE.

*Bracts.* 3 to 6; red with very narrow green margin along distal lip and narrow yellow margin on proximal lip; basal bract with green keel

*Rachis.* Red

*Sepals.* Green distally with white tip, white proximally

*Ovary.* White

*Pedicel.* White

VEGETATION.  Musoid; reddish stripe along lower midrib on some; margins undulate

*Heliconia stricta* Huber cv. Carli's Sharonii

BLOOMING. April through August

HEIGHT. 3 to 5 feet

HABITAT. Full sun to 50% shade

DISTRIBUTION. Uncertain [Costa Rica]

INFLORESCENCE.

*Bracts.* 5 to 6; red over cheek, extending onto keel distally, yellow at base and on proximal lip, green on distal lip and generally lighter green on proximal and medial keel; basal bracts with green along entire keel

*Rachis.* Yellow

*Sepals.* Green distally with white tip, white proximally

*Ovary.* White

*Pedicel.* White

VEGETATION. Musoid; maroon midrib above, maroon on lower blade surface with green midrib; leaf margins undulate

*Heliconia stricta* Huber cv. Castanza

BLOOMING.   July to November

HEIGHT.   3 to 4 feet

HABITAT.   Full sun to 30% shade

DISTRIBUTION.   Ecuador [Hawaii]

INFLORESCENCE.

*Bracts.*  3 to 5; pale pink on cheek, yellow at base, along keel and lip, green along median and distal lip and on tip; basal bract with green along distal keel

*Rachis.*  Yellow with green tint proximally

*Sepals.*  Green distally with small white tip, white proximally

*Ovary.*  White

*Pedicel.*  White

VEGETATION.   Musoid

*Heliconia stricta* Huber cv. Cochabamba

BLOOMING. July to November

HEIGHT. 4 to 6 feet

HABITAT. Full sun to 40% shade

DISTRIBUTION. Bolivia [Hawaii]

INFLORESCENCE.

*Bracts*. 4 to 5; red over most of bract, yellow on proximal keel and lip (increasing in area on upper bracts), green on distal lip and on tip; basal bract with green keel flecked with maroon

*Rachis*. Pink on sides and yellow on edges

*Sepals*. Primarily white, dark green distally with white tip

*Ovary*. White

*Pedicel*. White

VEGETATION. Musoid

*Heliconia stricta* Huber cv. Cooper's Sharonii

BLOOMING.    June to November

HEIGHT.    2 to 9 feet

HABITAT.    Full sun to 80% shade

DISTRIBUTION.    Bolivia [Florida, Hawaii]

INFLORESCENCE.

*Bracts.* 5 to 7; light red-orange over most of bract, yellow at base, thinly along lip, and on upper bracts along proximal keel, green thinly on margin of distal lip and on tip; basal bracts with more green

*Rachis.* Yellow, pink between basal bracts

*Sepals.* Dark green distally with white tip, white proximally

*Ovary.* White

*Pedicel.* White

VEGETATION.    Musoid; maroon midrib on upper surface, lower surface maroon with darker midrib; leaf margins slightly undulate

*Heliconia stricta* Huber cv. Dimples

BLOOMING.   August to December

HEIGHT.   2½ to 6 feet

HABITAT.   Full sun to 30% shade

DISTRIBUTION.   Uncertain [Hawaii, Costa Rica]

INFLORESCENCE.

*Bracts.* 3 to 5; pinkish-red at base and over most of bract, thin yellow along lip, changing to light green distally and on tip, light yellow along keel; basal and second bract with light green keel

*Rachis.* Light green and yellow on lower rachis and light yellow on upper

*Sepals.* Dark green distally with white tip, white proximally

*Ovary.* White

*Pedicel.* White

VEGETATION.   Musoid

*Heliconia stricta* Huber cv. Dorado Gold

BLOOMING.  October to December

HEIGHT.  3 to 5 feet

HABITAT.  Full sun to 40% shade

DISTRIBUTION.  Ecuador [Costa Rica]

INFLORESCENCE.

*Bracts.* 5 to 6; yellow over most of bract, small elongated slash of light pink on distal cheek (lacking on basal bract), narrow green band on lip to tip; basal bract and second bract with green keel

*Rachis.* Yellow

*Sepals.* Dark green distally with white tip, white proximally

*Ovary.* White

*Pedicel.* White

VEGETATION.  Musoid

*Heliconia stricta* Huber cv. Dwarf Jamaican

BLOOMING.  All year

HEIGHT.  1 to 3½ feet

HABITAT.  Full sun to 60% shade

DISTRIBUTION.  Uncertain [Florida, Hawaii, Costa Rica]

INFLORESCENCE.

*Bracts.* 3 to 5; red or pink with green stripe along keel and on tip, very narrow green stripe above and ma-roon stripe below along lip

*Rachis.* Red to pink to cream

*Sepals.* Green distally with white tip and white below

*Ovary.* White

*Pedicel.* White

VEGETATION.  Musoid; upper surface with red midrib, lower with paler red stripes along sides of midrib; margins undulate

*Heliconia stricta* Huber cv. Dwarf Wag

BLOOMING.   October to December

HEIGHT.   2 to 4 feet

HABITAT.   Full sun to 30% shade

DISTRIBUTION.   Ecuador [Costa Rica]

INFLORESCENCE.

*Bracts.* 6 to 8; red-pink on cheek, green on keel, lip, and tip; yellow at upper base, yellow-cream at lower base

*Rachis.* Yellow-cream

*Sepals.* Green on distal third with white tip and white below

*Ovary.* White

*Pedicel.* White

VEGETATION.   Musoid; usually maroon over most of upper midrib; lower midrib variable, maroon along sides of most of midrib or maroon spots at petiole only

*Heliconia stricta* Huber cv. Fire Bird

BLOOMING.   October to December

HEIGHT.   3 to 5 feet

HABITAT.   Full sun to 30% shade

DISTRIBUTION.   Ecuador [Florida, Hawaii, Costa Rica]

INFLORESCENCE.

*Bracts.* 6 to 7; red on base and cheek, green on keel and lip with narrow maroon stripe between green and red

*Rachis.* Dark red or maroon between lower bracts and red between upper bracts

*Sepals.* Green distally with small white tip, white proximally

*Ovary.* White

*Pedicel.* White

VEGETATION.   Musoid; maroon on upper midrib and along sides of lower midrib

*Heliconia stricta* Huber cv. Las Cruces

BLOOMING. December to September

HEIGHT. 3 to 5 feet

HABITAT. 20 to 60% shade

DISTRIBUTION. Unknown [Florida, Costa Rica]

INFLORESCENCE.

*Bracts.* 4 to 6; red over most of bract with narrow green and yellow lines along lip, and a green keel on basal bract

*Rachis.* Red

*Sepals.* Green distally with white tip and white below

*Ovary.* White

*Pedicel.* White

VEGETATION. Musoid; upper and lower midrib with red to maroon stripes; margins slightly undulate

*Heliconia stricta* Huber cv. Lee Moore

BLOOMING.   August to January

HEIGHT.   2 to 4 feet

HABITAT.   Full sun to 40% shade

DISTRIBUTION.   Peru [Florida]

INFLORESCENCE.

*Bracts.* 3 to 5; red, usually with thin yellow lip; basal bract with green keel

*Rachis.* Red at basal bract, reddish or yellow between upper bracts

*Sepals.* Dark green distally with white tip, white proximally

*Ovary.* White

*Pedicel.* White

VEGETATION.   Musoid; maroon stripe on upper and lower midrib, petiole maroon

*Heliconia stricta* Huber cv. Oliveira's Sharonii

BLOOMING.    April through January; peak around December

HEIGHT.    2 to 9 feet

HABITAT.    Full sun to 80% shade

DISTRIBUTION.    Uncertain [Florida, Costa Rica]

INFLORESCENCE.

*Bracts.* 5 to 6; red over cheek, yellow at base, on proximal lip, extending under green lip distally and on keel; green on medial and distal lip to tip, maroon on distal keel; basal bract with green keel

*Rachis.* Yellow

*Sepals.* Green distally with white tip, white proximally

*Ovary.* White

*Pedicel.* White

VEGETATION.    Musoid; midrib maroon above and below, lower blade surface maroon

*Heliconia stricta* Huber cv. Petite

BLOOMING.   October to December

HEIGHT.   2 to 3½ feet

HABITAT.   Full sun to 40% shade

DISTRIBUTION.   Ecuador [Costa Rica]

INFLORESCENCE.

*Bracts.* 3 to 4; pink-orange over most of bract, red extending out from base, green on lip and keel, pale yellow beneath green on lip

*Rachis.* Dark red

*Sepals.* Dark green distally with white tip, white below

*Ovary.* White

*Pedicel.* White

VEGETATION.   Musoid

*Heliconia stricta* Huber cv. Tagami

BLOOMING.   Probably all year

HEIGHT.   5 to 11 feet

HABITAT.   Full sun to 40% shade

DISTRIBUTION.   Uncertain [Florida, Hawaii, Costa Rica]

INFLORESCENCE.

*Bracts.* 5 to 10; dark to bright red over most of cheek; yellow, orange, or gold at base and on proximal lip and keel, green on distal lip and keel (diminishing on upper bracts)

*Rachis.* Yellow or gold at upper bracts shading to green below

*Sepals.* Dark green distally with white tip, white below

*Ovary.* White

*Pedicel.* White

VEGETATION.   Musoid

*Heliconia lennartiana* Kress

BLOOMING.  February to May

HEIGHT.  6 to 9 feet

HABITAT.  Full sun to 30% shade

DISTRIBUTION.  Panama [Hawaii, Costa Rica]

INFLORESCENCE.

*Bracts.* 6 to 8; yellow-orange over most of cheek and proximal keel with pink at base extending onto rachis; narrow green band on lip; distal keel and tip of basal bract green
*Rachis.* Pink
*Sepals.* Medium to dark green distally (lighter on some), white below
*Ovary.* White
*Pedicel.* White

VEGETATION.  Musoid; upper midrib sometimes faint red

*Heliconia orthotricha* L. Anderss.
cv. Edge of Nite

BLOOMING.    All year

HEIGHT.    2½ to 16 feet

HABITAT.    Full sun to 50% shade

DISTRIBUTION.    Colombia to Peru [Florida, Hawaii, Costa Rica]

INFLORESCENCE.

*Bracts.*  8 to 14; crimson on proximal cheek (extending more distally on upper bracts), maroon on distal keel and cheek; pink at base on upper bracts, lip and tip green; green keel on basal bracts; surface usually with velvety hairs

*Rachis.*  Reddish, or pink grading to yellow and greenish or white

*Sepals.*  Dark green distally, white below; tip greenish or whitish on some

*Ovary.*  White

*Pedicel.*  White

VEGETATION.    Musoid

*Heliconia orthotricha* L. Anderss. cv. She

BLOOMING. Possibly all year

HEIGHT. To 6½ feet

HABITAT. Full sun to 30% shade

DISTRIBUTION. Ecuador [Hawaii, Costa Rica]

INFLORESCENCE.

*Bracts.* 5 to 7; rose-pink over most of bract, maroon-black line along distal lip overlaid with dark green line and narrow clear edge; basal bract with green keel; surface usually with velvety hairs

*Rachis.* Pink shading to white

*Sepals.* Green distally with tiny light green tip, white proximally

*Ovary.* White

*Pedicel.* White

VEGETATION. Musoid; maroon stem, maroon on proximal third of lower midrib

*Heliconia bourgaeana* Petersen

BLOOMING.  All year

HEIGHT.  4 to 18 feet

HABITAT.  Full sun to 50% shade

DISTRIBUTION.  Veracruz area of Mexico [Florida, Hawaii, Brazil, Costa Rica]

INFLORESCENCE.

*Bracts.* 6 to 17; red, pink, or crimson

*Rachis.* Red or pink

*Sepals.* Gold or yellow on distal third, pale green-yellow proximally

*Ovary.* White

*Pedicel.* White

VEGETATION.  Musoid

*Heliconia champneiana* Griggs cv. Maya Blood

BLOOMING.   December to March and August to September

HEIGHT.   7 to 13 feet

HABITAT.   Full sun to 40% shade

DISTRIBUTION.   Southern Mexico [Florida]

INFLORESCENCE.

*Bracts.* 6 to 15; dark to light red, often with orange on proximal cheek; basal bract often green

*Rachis.* Red to reddish-orange

*Sepals.* Orange distally, changing to yellowish-white proximally

*Ovary.* White

*Pedicel.* White

VEGETATION.   Musoid; lower surface often with red or maroon midrib

*Heliconia champneiana* Griggs cv. Maya Gold

BLOOMING. April to November

HEIGHT. 6 to 15 feet

HABITAT. 20 to 50% shade

DISTRIBUTION. Belize, Guatemala, and Honduras [Florida, Hawaii, Costa Rica]

INFLORESCENCE.

*Bracts.* 5 to 13; gold to yellow over most of bract with light to dark green along distal keel and at tip, some bracts with minute flecks of maroon; basal bract mostly green

*Rachis.* Gold to yellow

*Sepals.* Green distally and white below

*Ovary.* Pale yellow

*Pedicel.* White with yellow tint

VEGETATION. Musoid

*Heliconia champneiana* Griggs cv. Splash

BLOOMING. May to November

HEIGHT. 6 to 13 feet

HABITAT. Full sun to 40% shade

DISTRIBUTION. Belize, Guatemala, and Honduras [Florida, Hawaii, Brazil, Costa Rica]

INFLORESCENCE.

*Bracts.* 4 to 11; base color of yellow or gold suffused with spots and blotches of scarlet; tips of upper bracts green

*Rachis.* Yellowish with spots of scarlet

*Sepals.* Green distally, white below

*Ovary.* Pale yellow

*Pedicel.* White

VEGETATION. Musoid

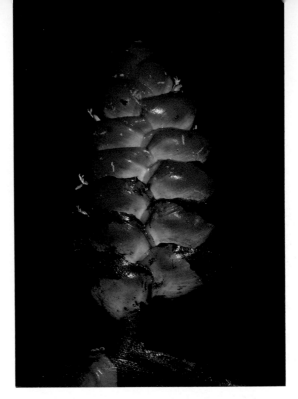

*Heliconia imbricata* (Kuntze) Baker

BLOOMING.    All year with peak in July and August

HEIGHT.    7 to 15 feet

HABITAT.    Full sun to 50% shade

DISTRIBUTION.    Nicaragua to Panama [Florida]

INFLORESCENCE.

*Bracts*.  12 to 28; ruby red over most of bract laterally, fading to pale pink-yellow near rachis and a pale green or green-yellow stripe along keel; usually a black (necrotic) line along lip

*Rachis*.  Cream

*Sepals*.  White with light green tip

*Ovary*.  Cream

*Pedicel*.  Cream

VEGETATION.    Musoid; leaves usually green, in some plants upper surface dark green with dark violet midrib and lower surface dark violet with violet midrib, especially when juvenile

*Heliconia imbricata* (Kuntze) Baker ×
*H. latispatha* Bentham cv. José Abalo

BLOOMING.    June to
September

HEIGHT.    6 to 18 feet

HABITAT.    Full sun to 40%
shade

DISTRIBUTION.    Costa Rica
[Florida, Hawaii, Costa Rica]

INFLORESCENCE.

*Bracts.* Primarily gold,
orange tint on lip and toward tips of upper bracts, a
pale pink flush on cheek

near axil; bracts tending to
be more yellow toward keel
and lower cheek

*Rachis.* Yellow with green
tint

*Sepals.* Pale olive green

*Ovary.* Light green on top
and cream below

*Pedicel.* Yellow-green

VEGETATION.    Musoid;
lower leaf surface sometimes
with light red near petiole

*Heliconia imbricata* (Kuntze) Baker ×
*H. sarapiquensis* Daniels & Stiles
cv. Harvey Bullis

BLOOMING.   June to November

HEIGHT.   7 to 12 feet

HABITAT.   Full sun to 40% shade

DISTRIBUTION.   Costa Rica [Hawaii]

INFLORESCENCE.

*Bracts.* 9 to 20; variable, red with orange flush on proximal keel and base; basal bract with green keel

*Rachis.* Yellow extending onto bract base

*Sepals.* Yellow to green

*Ovary.* White to yellow or light green

*Pedicel.* White, yellow, or yellow-green

VEGETATION.   Musoid; some with maroon stripe at base of lower midrib

*Heliconia reticulata* (Griggs) Winkler

BLOOMING. September to June with peak March to May

HEIGHT. 2½ to 5 feet

HABITAT. 30 to 75% shade

DISTRIBUTION. Costa Rica to Ecuador [Florida]

INFLORESCENCE.

*Bracts.* 10 to 18; red to pink, gradually turning black from tip with age

*Rachis.* Red to pink

*Sepals.* White with green distal margins

*Ovary.* Pink to red

*Pedicel.* White

VEGETATION. Musoid; upper leaf surface with fine bullate texture, midrib deep purple; lower surface similar with deep purple along veins

*Heliconia bella* Kress

BLOOMING.   December to August

HEIGHT.   3 to 6 feet

HABITAT.   50 to 75% shade

DISTRIBUTION.   Panama [Hawaii, Costa Rica]

INFLORESCENCE.

*Bracts.* 8 to 18; scarlet
*Rachis.* Pink and yellow

*Sepals.* Pale yellow at base to yellow at apex
*Ovary.* White to pale yellow
*Pedicel.* Pale yellow

VEGETATION.   Musoid; leaf blade dark green with burgundy red midrib above, and with distinctive reticulate venation below

*Heliconia atropurpurea* Daniels & Stiles

BLOOMING.    April to December

HEIGHT.    5 to 12 feet

HABITAT.    30 to 80% shade

DISTRIBUTION.    Costa Rica [Florida, Hawaii]

INFLORESCENCE.

*Bracts.* 10 to 15; dark red
*Rachis.* Red
*Sepals.* White, shading to pale green at tip

*Ovary.* White
*Pedicel.* White

VEGETATION.    Musoid; leaf color on lower surface variable, shiny deep maroon or liver colored with darker maroon midrib on smaller and younger leaves, with less intense maroon on older leaves and lacking on some

*Heliconia indica* var. *micholitzii* (Ridley) Kress

BLOOMING. Throughout the year

HEIGHT. 10 to 25 feet

HABITAT. Full sun to 50% shade

DISTRIBUTION. Bismarck Archipelago of Papua New Guinea [Florida, Hawaii]

INFLORESCENCE.

*Bracts.* 4 to 10; green to yellow-green at rachis

*Rachis.* Yellow-green with green speckles

*Sepals.* Green

*Ovary.* Yellow-green to orange; mature fruits red to orange

*Pedicel.* White

VEGETATION. Musoid

*Heliconia indica* Lamarck cv. Rabaul

BLOOMING.   Infrequently
HEIGHT.   4 to 8 feet
HABITAT.   Full sun
DISTRIBUTION.   Papua New Guinea [Florida, Hawaii]
INFLORESCENCE.
*Bracts.* 3 to 8; bright green

*Rachis.* Green
*Sepals.* Green
*Ovary.* Orange
*Pedicel.* Yellow
VEGETATION.   Musoid; bright yellow-green and somewhat succulent

*Heliconia indica* var. *rubricarpa* Kress

BLOOMING. Throughout the year

HEIGHT. 15 to 22 feet

HABITAT. Full sun to 50% shade

DISTRIBUTION. Papua New Guinea and the Bismarck Archipelago [Hawaii]

INFLORESCENCE.

*Bracts.* 8 to 11; green, some-times red near rachis

*Rachis.* Yellow-green with green speckles

*Sepals.* Pale green

*Ovary.* Light green; mature fruits red

*Pedicel.* White

VEGETATION. Musoid

*Heliconia indica* Lamarck cv. Spectabilis

BLOOMING.   Infrequently

HEIGHT.   10 to 20 feet

HABITAT.   Full sun to 50% shade

DISTRIBUTION.   Only known from cultivation, originally from South Pacific Islands [widely cultivated]

INFLORESCENCE.

*Bracts*.  4 to 8; pale green with thin red margins or mottled red and green

*Rachis*.  Pale yellow or green

*Sepals*.  Green becoming red with age

*Ovary*.  Pale orange becoming red with age

*Pedicel*.  Yellow or green

VEGETATION.   Musoid; two forms: (1) green above with variable shades of bronzy red below, (2) green or reddish with rose pink, red, or white lateral striations; both forms can sometimes be found on the same plant

*Heliconia indica* Lamarck cv. Striata

BLOOMING.    Infrequently

HEIGHT.    5 to 15 feet

HABITAT.    50% shade

DISTRIBUTION.    Known only from cultivation, originally from South Pacific Islands [Florida, Hawaii]

INFLORESCENCE.

*Bracts.*  4 to 7; green with white longitudinal markings, and some yellow near rachis

*Rachis.*  Green

*Sepals.*  Green

*Ovary.*  Orange

*Pedicel.*  Yellow-green

VEGETATION.    Musoid; leaf blades and petioles with distinctive white or yellow lateral striations above and below

*Heliconia papuana* Kress

BLOOMING.    Throughout the year

HEIGHT.    10 to 15 feet

HABITAT.    Full sun to 50% shade

DISTRIBUTION.    New Guinea [Hawaii, Costa Rica]

INFLORESCENCE.

*Bracts.* 6 to 10; green to yellow-green near rachis

*Rachis.* Yellow-green

*Sepals.* White to light green at tip

*Ovary.* Light yellow; mature fruits bright orange

*Pedicel.* White to yellow

VEGETATION.    Musoid

*Heliconia densiflora* Verlot cv. Fire Flash

BLOOMING.   All year

HEIGHT.   1½ to 5 feet

HABITAT.   Full sun to 40% shade

DISTRIBUTION.   Uncertain [Florida, Hawaii, Australia, Costa Rica]

INFLORESCENCE.

*Bracts.* 4 to 5; red or red-orange over most of bract with yellow-gold at base and proximal lip (increasing in area on upper bracts)

*Rachis.* Red, changing to yellow-gold on upper bracts

*Sepals.* Orange on distal ¾ shading to light yellow proximally, tip greenish

*Ovary.* Orange on distal half (with green spot at upper margin on older ovaries) and yellow proximally

*Pedicel.* Yellow

VEGETATION.   Musoid

*Heliconia psittacorum* L.f. cv. Andromeda

BLOOMING. All year

HEIGHT. 1½ to 9 feet

HABITAT. Full sun to 50% shade

DISTRIBUTION. Guyanas [widely cultivated]

INFLORESCENCE.

*Bracts.* 3 to 5; somewhat variable, outer surface orange to red, sometimes with green tint on keel, inner surface red shading to orange proximally

*Rachis.* Orange, orange with red infusion, or green

*Sepals.* Orange with distal metallic black or green band and orange tip

*Ovary.* Dark orange distally and light orange or orange-yellow below

*Pedicel.* Orange

VEGETATION. Musoid

*Heliconia psittacorum* L.f. cv. Black Cherry

BLOOMING.    All year

HEIGHT.    3 to 5 feet

HABITAT.    Full sun to 30% shade

DISTRIBUTION.    Uncertain [Hawaii]

INFLORESCENCE.

*Bracts.*  4 to 6; dark red shading on lower two bracts to maroon distally

*Rachis.* Pink distally shading to red proximally

*Sepals.* Green shading to dark green on distal third with darker green band and white tip

*Ovary.* Green on distal third and white proximally

*Pedicel.* White

VEGETATION.    Musoid

*Heliconia psittacorum* L.f. cv. Choconiana

BLOOMING.    All year

HEIGHT.    1 to 8 feet

HABITAT.    Full sun to 50% shade

DISTRIBUTION.    Guianas [widely cultivated]

INFLORESCENCE.

*Bracts*.  4 to 6; orange with pale green on outer tip of basal bract

*Rachis*.  Orange

*Sepals*.  Orange with distal dark green or black band and yellow-white tip

*Ovary*.  Bright orange distally and pale orange below

*Pedicel*.  Orange

VEGETATION.    Musoid

*Heliconia psittacorum* L.f. cv. Fuchsia

BLOOMING.   All year

HEIGHT.   4 to 6 feet

HABITAT.   Full sun to 30% shade

DISTRIBUTION.   Uncertain [Hawaii]

INFLORESCENCE.

*Bracts*.  4 to 5; fuchsia (reddish purple) with dusky area proximally

*Rachis*.  Fuchsia beneath basal bract to pale white-green on upper bracts

*Sepals*.  Light yellow-green with dark green band distally and whitish tip

*Ovary*.  Dark green on distal fifth and light green proximally

*Pedicel*.  White

VEGETATION.   Musoid

*Heliconia psittacorum* L.f. cv. Kathy

BLOOMING.  All year

HEIGHT.  4 to 6 feet

HABITAT.  Full sun to 30% shade

DISTRIBUTION.  Uncertain [Hawaii]

INFLORESCENCE.

*Bracts.*  4 to 5; dark red with small cream patch at basal lip; basal bract with thin distal green keel

*Rachis.*  Dark red, lighter on upper rachis

*Sepals.*  Orange with distal black-green band and white to orange tip

*Ovary.*  Orange with light yellow at base

*Pedicel.*  Dull green at distal end and orange proximally

VEGETATION.  Musoid

*Heliconia psittacorum* L.f. cv. Lady Di

BLOOMING. April to November

HEIGHT. 2½ to 5 feet

HABITAT. Full sun to 40% shade

DISTRIBUTION. Uncertain [Florida, Hawaii, Barbados, Costa Rica]

INFLORESCENCE.

*Bracts*. 5 to 8; dark red with paler red on lower cheek

*Rachis*. Red, pink, or pale pink

*Sepals*. Light yellow with distal dark green band and white tip

*Ovary*. Yellow, some proximally cream

*Pedicel*. Light yellow or cream

VEGETATION. Musoid

*Heliconia psittacorum* L.f. cv. Lillian

BLOOMING.   May to August

HEIGHT.   2½ to 5 feet

HABITAT.   Full sun to 30% shade

DISTRIBUTION.   Guyana [Costa Rica]

INFLORESCENCE.

*Bracts*. 4 to 7; pink proximally shading to red distally; basal bract with green tip

*Rachis*. Pink to light red

*Sepals*. Yellow with distal blue-green band or blotches and yellow tip

*Ovary*. Green distally and green-yellow proximally

*Pedicel*. Pale yellow to cream

VEGETATION.   Musoid

*Heliconia psittacorum* L.f. cv. Parakeet

BLOOMING.   May to July

HEIGHT.   3 to 6 feet

HABITAT.   Full sun to 40% shade

DISTRIBUTION.   Uncertain [Florida, Hawaii, Costa Rica]

INFLORESCENCE.

*Bracts.* 4 to 5; dark red to pink distally with pale green or cream-yellow proximally

*Rachis.* Pale green (with or without yellow tint) or cream

*Sepals.* Yellow (sometimes orange) with distal dark green band and white or yellow tip

*Ovary.* Green

*Pedicel.* Light green distally and cream proximally

VEGETATION.   Musoid

*Heliconia psittacorum* L.f. cv. Peter Bacon

BLOOMING.  September and October

HEIGHT.  2½ to 5 feet

HABITAT.  Full sun to 30% shade

DISTRIBUTION.  Brazil [Florida]

INFLORESCENCE.

*Bracts.*  3 to 5; green prox-imally shading to cream and pink distally

*Rachis.*  Green

*Sepals.*  Orange with distal black band and white tip

*Ovary.*  Yellow

*Pedicel.*  Yellow to yellow-green

VEGETATION.  Musoid

*Heliconia psittacorum* L.f. cv. St. Vincent Red

BLOOMING.    All year with peak March to October

HEIGHT.    2½ to 6 feet

HABITAT.    Full sun to 40% shade

DISTRIBUTION.    St. Vincent [Florida, Hawaii, Brazil, Costa Rica]

INFLORESCENCE.

*Bracts.*  4 to 6; bright to deep red over most of bract shading to orange proximally

*Rachis.*  Orange distally shading to reddish proximally

*Sepals.*  Orange with generally indistinct green-black area distally (but not a defined band)

*Ovary.*  Orange on top and distal ⅔ with pale orange or yellow proximally

*Pedicel.*  Orange

VEGETATION.    Musoid

*Heliconia psittacorum* L.f. cv. Sassy

BLOOMING.   April to November

HEIGHT.   3 to 6 feet

HABITAT.   Full sun to 40% shade

DISTRIBUTION.   Uncertain [widely cultivated]

INFLORESCENCE.

*Bracts.* 4 to 6; pale green or cream on proximal half and red or pink distally; basal bract with narrow green keel and green tip

*Rachis.* Pale white or green

*Sepals.* Orange with distal green-black band and white tip

*Ovary.* Green distally and yellow-green proximally

*Pedicel.* Yellow-green or pale green

VEGETATION.   Musoid

*Heliconia psittacorum* L.f. cv. Shamrock

BLOOMING.  January to March

HEIGHT.  3 to 5 feet

HABITAT.  Full sun to 30% shade

DISTRIBUTION.  Uncertain [Brazil]

INFLORESCENCE.

*Bracts.*  5 to 7; dark to dull green from base shading to pale pink along distal lip and on tip, except basal bract with green tip

*Rachis.*  Green or green-yellow

*Sepals.*  Orange with green-black distal band and white tip

*Ovary.*  Dark green on distal half and green-white proximally

*Pedicel.*  Pale green

VEGETATION.  Musoid

*Heliconia psittacorum* L.f. cv. Strawberries and Cream

BLOOMING. All year

HEIGHT. 3 to 5 feet

HABITAT. Full sun to 30% shade

DISTRIBUTION. Uncertain [Hawaii]

INFLORESCENCE.

*Bracts.* 3 to 5; strawberry red-pink distally and cream proximally; basal bracts mostly red-pink with a thin distal green keel

*Rachis.* Cream with green tint

*Sepals.* Pale yellow with distal dark green band and white tip

*Ovary.* Pale yellow with green spot on distal corner

*Pedicel.* Cream with green tint

VEGETATION. Musoid

*Heliconia psittacorum* L.f. cv. Suriname Sassy

BLOOMING.  All year

HEIGHT.  3 to 4 feet

HABITAT.  Full sun to 30% shade

DISTRIBUTION.  Suriname [Costa Rica]

INFLORESCENCE.

*Bracts.* 5 to 6; dull yellow or pale green at base, shading to yellow with pink infusions distally; basal bract with distal green keel and tip

*Rachis.* Yellow with green and/or pink infusions

*Sepals.* Orange with dark green distal band and small dusky white tip

*Ovary.* Orange distally and yellow proximally

*Pedicel.* Orange to cream

VEGETATION.  Musoid

*Heliconia psittacorum* L.f. × *H. spathocircinata*
Aristeguieta cv. Alan Carle

BLOOMING.   April to August

HEIGHT.   3 to 5 feet

HABITAT.   Full sun to 20% shade

DISTRIBUTION.   Grenada [Florida, Costa Rica]

INFLORESCENCE.

*Bracts.* 3 to 6; reddish on most of cheek and keel, shading to yellowish on proximal cheek and along lip; basal bract with green along keel and on tip

*Rachis.* Greenish to yellow

*Sepals.* Dark green on distal third with light tip, yellow on proximal part

*Ovary.* Yellow

*Pedicel.* Cream or yellowish

VEGETATION.   Musoid

*Heliconia psittacorum* L.f. × *H. spathocircinata*
Aristeguieta cv. Golden Torch

BLOOMING.    All year

HEIGHT.    2½ to 9 feet

HABITAT.    Full sun to 40% shade

DISTRIBUTION.    Guyana [widely cultivated]

INFLORESCENCE.

*Bracts.* 4 to 8; golden or yellow; basal bract with green keel and tip

*Rachis.* Golden, often with small red area at base

*Sepals.* Golden with faint green tip

*Ovary.* Golden on distal third and top, yellow below

*Pedicel.* Yellow with green tint

VEGETATION.    Musoid

*Heliconia psittacorum* L.f. × *H. spathocircinata*
Aristeguieta cv. Golden Torch Adrian

BLOOMING.   January to
October

HEIGHT.   3½ to 5 feet

HABITAT.   Full sun to 20%
shade

DISTRIBUTION.   Guyana
[Florida, Hawaii, Costa Rica,
Venezuela]

INFLORESCENCE.

*Bracts.* 5 to 7; maroon to
dark red at base; distal half
of upper bracts with yellow
and splashes of red; basal
bract with faint green keel

*Rachis.* Maroon to dark red,
or yellow on light red

*Sepals.* Golden with faint
green distally

*Ovary.* Bright yellow on tip
and yellow with flush of
green or dull green below

*Pedicel.* Green-yellow

VEGETATION.   Musoid

*Heliconia* × *nickeriensis* Maas & deRooij
(*H. psittacorum* × *H. marginata*)

BLOOMING. June to
November

HEIGHT. 4 to 10 feet

HABITAT. Full sun to 40%
shade

DISTRIBUTION. Guyana
and Suriname [widely
cultivated]

INFLORESCENCE.

*Bracts.* 5 to 9; pink-red over
most of keel and cheek, and
yellow on lip and tip and
small part of base

*Rachis.* Usually yellow
distally and pink below

*Sepals.* Gold

*Ovary.* Dark yellow distally
and light yellow below

*Pedicel.* Light yellow

VEGETATION. Musoid

*Heliconia acuminata* L.C. Richard cv. Cheri R

BLOOMING.    December to April

HEIGHT.    2½ to 3½ feet

HABITAT.    Full sun to 30% shade

DISTRIBUTION.    Uncertain [Brazil]

INFLORESCENCE.

*Bracts.*  4 to 6; bright orange to red-orange

*Rachis.*  Bright orange to red-orange

*Sepals.*  Yellow-orange, some with very faint dark green distal band

*Ovary.*  Dark orange

*Pedicel.*  Light orange

VEGETATION.    Musoid

*Heliconia acuminata* L.C. Richard cv. Ruby

BLOOMING.   May to December

HEIGHT.   3½ to 6 feet

HABITAT.   20 to 50% shade

DISTRIBUTION.   Guyana [Florida, Costa Rica, Venezuela]

INFLORESCENCE.

*Bracts.*  4 to 6; red with pink at base or entirely pink

*Rachis.*  Pink above and red below

*Sepals.*  Distal end with metallic-blue or blue-green band and white tip; proximally pale, dark green or cream

*Ovary.*  Dark green distally and light green basally, or entirely cream

*Pedicel.*  Light green or cream

VEGETATION.   Musoid; stem may be maroon or red blotched, usually with maroon all along lower midrib

*Heliconia acuminata* L.C. Richard cv. Taruma

BLOOMING.   October

HEIGHT.   2 to 3 feet

HABITAT.   20% shade

DISTRIBUTION.   Brazil [Hawaii]

INFLORESCENCE.

*Bracts.*  5 to 6; red
*Rachis.*  Dark red
*Sepals.*  White with distal green-black band and white tip
*Ovary.*  White with small green spots on distal three angles
*Pedicel.*  White with green tint near base

VEGETATION.   Musoid; maroon on stem, petiole, and lower midrib

*Heliconia acuminata* L.C. Richard cv. Yellow Waltz

BLOOMING.  October

HEIGHT.  3 to 4 feet

HABITAT.  Full sun to 30% shade

DISTRIBUTION.  Brazil [Hawaii]

INFLORESCENCE.

*Bracts.* 5 to 6; yellow with green infusion along cheek; basal bract (possibly others) entirely green on old inflorescences

*Rachis.* Yellow

*Sepals.* Yellow with distal green-black band and dusky white tip

*Ovary.* Yellow (turning greenish with age)

*Pedicel.* Yellow (turning greenish with age)

VEGETATION.  Musoid; lower midrib slightly maroon on some; white waxy coating on lower surface of leaf blade

*slightly spiral

*Heliconia angusta* Vellozo cv. Holiday

BLOOMING.   August to March (variable)

HEIGHT.   2 to 4 feet

HABITAT.   20 to 80% shade

DISTRIBUTION.   Southeast Brazil [Florida, Hawaii, Costa Rica, Venezuela]

INFLORESCENCE.

*Bracts.*  4 to 8; red, pinkish-red, or pink; basal bract with green on distal keel and tip

*Rachis.* Red to pink-red

*Sepals.* White with green tint on distal fourth

*Ovary.* Red, yellowish-red distally

*Pedicel.* Red

VEGETATION.   Musoid

*Heliconia angusta* Vellozo cv. Orange Christmas

BLOOMING.   January to July

HEIGHT.   4 to 10 feet

HABITAT.   20 to 50% shade

DISTRIBUTION.   Southeast Brazil [Florida, Hawaii, Costa Rica, Venezuela]

INFLORESCENCE.

*Bracts.* 7 to 11; orange with greenish-yellow tint along lip and on tip

*Rachis.* Orange

*Sepals.* White with green tint distally and yellow tint basally

*Ovary.* Yellow

*Pedicel.* Yellow

VEGETATION.   Musoid

*Heliconia angusta* Vellozo cv. Yellow Christmas

BLOOMING.  February and March

HEIGHT.  4 to 7 feet

HABITAT.  Full sun to 50% shade

DISTRIBUTION.  Southeast Brazil [Florida, Hawaii, Costa Rica, Venezuela]

INFLORESCENCE.

*Bracts.*  5 to 9; yellow

*Rachis.*  Yellow

*Sepals.*  White with green tint distally and yellow tint basally

*Ovary.*  Yellow with pale green on top

*Pedicel.*  Yellow

VEGETATION.  Musoid

*Heliconia gracilis* Daniels & Stiles
cv. Gil Daniels

BLOOMING.  November to June with peak March to April

HEIGHT.  1½ to 4 feet

HABITAT.  20 to 60% shade

DISTRIBUTION.  Costa Rica [Florida, Hawaii]

INFLORESCENCE.

*Bracts.*  4 to 5; red; basal

bract usually with green keel and leaflet at tip

*Rachis.*  Yellow with dark orange or scarlet

*Sepals.*  Pale yellow to creamy-white

*Ovary.*  Yellow-green

*Pedicel.*  White

VEGETATION.  Musoid

*Heliconia gracilis* Daniels & Stiles cv. John Hall

BLOOMING.   All year, primarily December to February

HEIGHT.   1½ to 5½ feet

HABITAT.   30 to 60% shade

DISTRIBUTION.   Costa Rica [Florida]

INFLORESCENCE.

*Bracts.*  3 to 7; yellow, basal bract with green keel and tip and on some a green leaflet

*Rachis.*  Yellow

*Sepals.*  Pale yellow on distal half and white below

*Ovary.*  Green

*Pedicel.*  White

VEGETATION.   Musoid

*Heliconia ignescens* Daniels & Stiles

BLOOMING.   Peak July to August and into November

HEIGHT.   1½ to 4½ feet

HABITAT.   20 to 50% shade

DISTRIBUTION.   Costa Rica and Panama [Florida, Hawaii]

INFLORESCENCE.

*Bracts.* 4 to 8; orange shading to gold on distal ends; basal bract with more gold along cheek and with green on keel and tip

*Rachis.* Orange shading to gold

*Sepals.* Yellow

*Ovary.* Yellow-green

*Pedicel.* Yellow to white

VEGETATION.   Musoid

*Heliconia rodriguezii* Stiles

BLOOMING. All year with peak April and May

HEIGHT. 2 to 5 feet

HABITAT. 30 to 60% shade

DISTRIBUTION. Costa Rica [Florida]

INFLORESCENCE.

*Bracts.* 3 to 5; scarlet to red

*Rachis.* Red

*Sepals.* Yellow

*Ovary.* Pale yellow

*Pedicel.* Pale yellow

VEGETATION. Musoid

*Heliconia lasiorachis* L. Anderss.

BLOOMING.    April to November

HEIGHT.    1½ to 9 feet

HABITAT.    Full sun to 30% shade

DISTRIBUTION.    Colombia, Peru, and western Brazil [Hawaii, Costa Rica]

INFLORESCENCE.

*Bracts.* 3 to 5; cherry red with small light green area at base; basal bract with green tip or leaflet

*Rachis.* Light yellow-green

*Sepals.* Light green with dark green irregular band distally and with a light tip

*Ovary.* Dark green on distal half and light green proximally

*Pedicel.* Light green

VEGETATION.    Musoid

*Heliconia aemygdiana* Burle-Marx
ssp. *transandina* L. Anderss.

BLOOMING.   June to August

HEIGHT.   3 to 6 feet

HABITAT.   Full sun to 30% shade

DISTRIBUTION.   Western Ecuador [Costa Rica]

INFLORESCENCE.

*Bracts.* 5 to 10; dark red with mottled orange on proximal cheek

*Rachis.* Red or reddish-orange

*Sepals.* Green

*Ovary.* Yellow

*Pedicel.* Yellow

VEGETATION.   Musoid

*Heliconia lingulata* Ruiz & Pavón cv. Fan

BLOOMING.   All year, with spring and late summer peaks in some areas

HEIGHT.   5 to 17 feet

HABITAT.   Full sun to 40% shade

DISTRIBUTION.   Peru to Bolivia [Florida, Hawaii, Barbados, Brazil, Costa Rica]

INFLORESCENCE.

*Bracts.* 7 to 27; variable; yellow to yellow-green on cheeks with light red to orange on distal parts of lower bracts

*Rachis.* Yellow or yellow-green

*Sepals.* Pale green-yellow, or yellow

*Ovary.* Pale green distally and pale yellow proximally (turning bright green distally with age)

*Pedicel.* Green-yellow

VEGETATION.   Musoid

*Heliconia librata* Griggs

BLOOMING.   May to December

HEIGHT.   4 to 10 feet

HABITAT.   Full sun to 40% shade

DISTRIBUTION.   Mexico to Nicaragua [Florida, Hawaii, Costa Rica]

INFLORESCENCE.

*Bracts.* 11 to 18; yellow; basal bract with green keel and tip; some populations with orange infusions over bracts, especially in younger inflorescences

*Rachis.* Yellow

*Sepals.* Green with yellow tint toward base and tip

*Ovary.* Dark green on distal ⅔ and yellow-green below

*Pedicel.* Dull yellow

VEGETATION.   Musoid

*Heliconia clinophila* R.R. Smith

BLOOMING.   All year

HEIGHT.   5 to 10 feet

HABITAT.   Full sun to 40% shade

DISTRIBUTION.   Costa Rica and Panama [Florida]

INFLORESCENCE.

*Bracts.* 6 to 10; yellow over most of bract with greenish keel

*Rachis.* Greenish to yellowish

*Sepals.* Light green with pale yellow proximally

*Ovary.* Green distally and pale yellow proximally

*Pedicel.* Green

VEGETATION.   Musoid

*Heliconia velloziana* L. Emygdio

BLOOMING.   January to April

HEIGHT.   6 to 15 feet

HABITAT.   50% shade

DISTRIBUTION.   Brazil [Hawaii]

INFLORESCENCE.

*Bracts.*  7-14; red, upper bracts with gold at base; basal bracts with green keel and tip

*Rachis.*  Gold to red

*Sepals.*  Green, proximally yellow-green

*Ovary.*  Light yellow

*Pedicel.*  Light yellow

VEGETATION.   Musoid

*Heliconia zebrina* Plowman, Kress & Kennedy
cv. Inca

BLOOMING.    March to July
HEIGHT.    2 to 4 feet
HABITAT.    20 to 70% shade
DISTRIBUTION.    Peru [Florida, Hawaii, Costa Rica]

INFLORESCENCE.

*Bracts.* 5 to 7; red-orange (to pink-orange on older bracts)
*Rachis.* Red

*Sepals.* Green
*Ovary.* Dark green
*Pedicel.* Light green

VEGETATION.    Musoid; upper surface of leaf blades with 6 to 9 dark green bars extending laterally out from midrib (resembling leaves of *Calathea zebrina*); lower surface green or maroon

*Heliconia zebrina* Plowman, Kress & Kennedy
cv. Tim Plowman

BLOOMING.   September

HEIGHT.   To 4 feet

HABITAT.   Full sun to 80% shade

DISTRIBUTION.   Peru [Florida, Brazil]

INFLORESCENCE.

*Bracts.* 5 to 7; red; upper bracts with small white patch at base
*Rachis.* Red

*Sepals.* Light green on distal third to white proximally
*Ovary.* Light green on distal half to white proximally
*Pedicel.* White

VEGETATION.   Musoid; upper surface dark green with contrasting greenish-white midrib, lower surface maroon with darker maroon midrib

*Heliconia lankesteri* Standley var. *lankesteri*

BLOOMING.   All year with peak from December to March

HEIGHT.   7 to 12 feet

HABITAT.   30 to 80% shade

DISTRIBUTION.   Costa Rica and Panama [Florida]

INFLORESCENCE.

*Bracts.* 10 to 17; yellow with varying shades of green on keel, sometimes with red on cheek

*Rachis.* Yellow

*Sepals.* Greenish or yellow-green on distal ⅔ to white basally

*Ovary.* Green

*Pedicel.* Cream, pale yellow-green or white, some with scarlet distally

VEGETATION.   Musoid

*Heliconia lankesteri* var. *rubra* Daniels & Stiles

BLOOMING.   Possibly all year with peak January to April

HEIGHT.   6 to 12 feet

HABITAT.   20 to 60% shade

DISTRIBUTION.   Costa Rica and Panama [Florida]

INFLORESCENCE.

*Bracts.* 8 to 17; red, some shading from dark red at tip to orange at base

*Rachis.* Gold to red

*Sepals.* Yellow with green tint distally

*Ovary.* Green

*Pedicel.* Yellow-pink

VEGETATION.   Musoid; lower surface with dark maroon midrib

*Heliconia lophocarpa* Daniels & Stiles

BLOOMING.   July to January

HEIGHT.   3 to 8 feet

HABITAT.   Full sun to 40% shade

DISTRIBUTION.   Costa Rica and Panama [Florida]

INFLORESCENCE.

*Bracts.* 13 to 26; red with black coriaceous lip and tip, progressing upward from lower bract with age

*Rachis.* Red

*Sepals.* White

*Ovary.* Pink with sepals attached, turning red with age

*Pedicel.* Pink, becoming darker with age

VEGETATION.   Musoid; upper surface with maroon midrib and raised lateral veins; lower surface with purple tint and purple midrib extending onto stem

*Heliconia episcopalis* Vellozo

BLOOMING. All year

HEIGHT. 2½ to 7 feet

HABITAT. Full sun to 70% shade

DISTRIBUTION. Throughout Amazonian South America and eastern Brazil [Florida, Hawaii, Costa Rica]

INFLORESCENCE.

*Bracts.* 18 to 24; lower bracts with red on proximal ⅔ shading to orange-yellow with yellow-green tip; upper bracts nearly all yellow or orange, basally green on some with a narrow yellow lip

*Rachis.* Orange to yellow

*Sepals.* Orange distally and clear yellow on proximal ⅔ to ¾

*Ovary.* Light orange

*Pedicel.* Pale yellow

VEGETATION. Musoid

*Heliconia* × *flabellata* Abalo & Morales
(*H. episcopalis* × *H. standleyi*)

BLOOMING.    October to
May

HEIGHT.    12 to 16 feet

HABITAT.    Full sun to 30%
shade

DISTRIBUTION.    Ecuador
[Costa Rica, Brazil]

INFLORESCENCE.

*Bracts.*  12 to 18; red proximally and yellow distally;

basal bract green-yellow
distally

*Rachis.*  Maroon on basal
bract; upper bracts red, with
pink and white

*Sepals.*  Pale green to yellow
on distal third, pale white-
yellow on medial third and
white on proximal third

*Ovary.*  White

*Pedicel.*  White

VEGETATION.    Musoid

*some nodding

*Heliconia calatheaphylla* Daniels & Stiles

BLOOMING.    May to July

HEIGHT.    3 to 9 feet

HABITAT.    20 to 90% shade

DISTRIBUTION.    Costa Rica [Florida]

INFLORESCENCE.

*Bracts*.  3 to 4; variable, green shading to yellow at base or white shading to yellow toward tip of basal bract and yellow around keel of basal bract, extending onto rachis, often turning dark green with age

*Rachis*.  Yellow to yellow-green

*Sepals*.  Greenish-yellow (greener toward tip, yellowish toward ovary); older sepals with more yellow

*Ovary*.  Green on distal fourth and on top, yellow below

*Pedicel*.  Yellow

VEGETATION.    Cannoid; blade texture unique, lateral veins on upper surface raised and rigid (like a *Calathea*)

*Heliconia subulata* Ruiz & Pavón

BLOOMING.   January to November

HEIGHT.   4 to 9 feet

HABITAT.   Full sun to 60% shade

DISTRIBUTION.   Ecuador to Argentina and southern Brazil [Florida, Hawaii, Costa Rica, Venezuela]

INFLORESCENCE.

*Bracts.*  4 to 11; red or rose-pink at base shading to rose to maroon along lip and at tip; basal bract with green stripe along keel, on lower cheek, and on tip; second and third bracts with green tip

*Rachis.*  Red or rose (darker toward inflorescence base)

*Sepals.*  Yellow-green with green on distal third to fourth

*Ovary.*  Maroon on distal half and red below

*Pedicel.*  Red

VEGETATION.   Cannoid; lower midrib may have narrow red stripe

*Heliconia metallica* Planchon & Linden
ex Hooker

BLOOMING. All year

HEIGHT. 4 to 8 feet

HABITAT. Full sun to 60% shade

DISTRIBUTION. Widespread, Honduras to Bolivia [widely cultivated]

INFLORESCENCE.

*Bracts.* 5 to 7; red to green, if red, basal bract with green stripe along keel and on tip
*Rachis.* Red to green
*Sepals.* Red to pink with small white or pale area around tip
*Ovary.* Maroon to black on top; white below
*Pedicel.* White, some with pink at ovary

VEGETATION. Cannoid; midrib white on upper surface of most leaves, sometimes light green or green, maroon on lower surface with darker midrib on most leaves, but sometimes only green

*Heliconia osaënsis* Cufodontis

BLOOMING.  December to June

HEIGHT.  4 to 13 feet

HABITAT.  Full sun to 30% shade

DISTRIBUTION.  Costa Rica and Panama [Florida, Brazil]

INFLORESCENCE.

*Bracts.* 5 to 12; orange to red
*Rachis.* Red

*Sepals.* Orange with tip yellow, yellow-green, or green
*Ovary.* Maroon on top and reddish-white below becoming dark green on top and red below after sepal drop
*Pedicel.* Pink and cream or orange

VEGETATION.  Cannoid; lower surface of leaf blade always green

*Heliconia wilsonii* Daniels & Stiles

BLOOMING. All year with peak September to November

HEIGHT. 5 to 15 feet

HABITAT. 20 to 50% shade

DISTRIBUTION. Costa Rica and Panama [Florida]

INFLORESCENCE.

*Bracts.* 6 to 9; red, yellow at base of distal bracts on some, turning orange-red on older bracts; basal bract usually with green distal keel, tip, and leaflet

*Rachis.* Red

*Sepals.* Yellow

*Ovary.* Red, turning red-black on top of some older ovaries

*Pedicel.* Yellow with red tint, reddish-yellow on some

VEGETATION. Cannoid

*Heliconia vaginalis* Bentham

BLOOMING.   June to December with peak in September

HEIGHT.   3 to 15 feet

HABITAT.   Full sun to 40% shade

DISTRIBUTION.   Costa Rica to Colombia [Florida, Hawaii]

INFLORESCENCE.

*Bracts.* 3 to 7; red to red-orange, basal bract may have distal green keel and tip or leaflet

*Rachis.* Red to crimson

*Sepals.* Yellow with green on distal third

*Ovary.* Green on distal third and top and yellow below

*Pedicel.* Yellow

VEGETATION.   Cannoid

*sometimes slightly spiral

*Heliconia mathiasiae* Daniels & Stiles cv. Mildred

BLOOMING.    All year with peak September to November

HEIGHT.    1½ to 15 feet

HABITAT.    Full sun to 80% shade

DISTRIBUTION.    Costa Rica and Nicaragua [Florida, Hawaii, Brazil]

INFLORESCENCE.

*Bracts.*  3 to 9; red, some with orange tint near base; basal bract usually with green keel, tip, and leaflet

*Rachis.*  Red

*Sepals.*  Yellow, often with red near ovary

*Ovary.*  Dark red to crimson on top and distal half, shading to lighter red below

*Pedicel.*  Red to pink

VEGETATION.    Zingiberoid

*Heliconia mathiasiae* Daniels & Stiles cv. Pacal

BLOOMING.  All year

HEIGHT.  3 to 14 feet

HABITAT.  Full sun to 50% shade

DISTRIBUTION.  Southern Mexico to Nicaragua [Florida, Hawaii]

INFLORESCENCE.

*Bracts.* 5 to 6; dark red to red-orange; basal bract usu-ally with distal green keel and tip and leaflet

*Rachis.* Red

*Sepals.* Yellow with light to dark green on distal third

*Ovary.* Light to dark green distally and yellow below

*Pedicel.* Yellow, some with pink tint

VEGETATION.  Zingiberoid

*Heliconia hirsuta* L.f. cv. Alicia

BLOOMING.    June to March

HEIGHT.    3 to 8 feet

HABITAT.    Full sun to 50% shade

DISTRIBUTION.    Honduras [Florida, Brazil]

INFLORESCENCE.

*Bracts.*  3 to 6; orange, lower two bracts with green tips, some bracts slightly red on distal half

*Rachis.*  Green to dark green

*Sepals.*  Orange with distal dark green band and white tip

*Ovary.*  Green, dark green on distal half with red apex

*Pedicel.*  Light green

VEGETATION.    Zingiberoid

*Heliconia hirsuta* L.f. cv. Costa Flores

BLOOMING.   June to September

HEIGHT.   3 to 6 feet

HABITAT.   Full sun to 30% shade

DISTRIBUTION.   Uncertain [Costa Rica]

INFLORESCENCE.

*Bracts*.  6 to 8; red

*Rachis*.  Red

*Sepals*.  Yellow with black band distally, tip white

*Ovary*.  Red on distal half and yellow below

*Pedicel*.  Yellow

VEGETATION.   Zingiberoid

*Heliconia hirsuta* L.f. cv. Darrell

BLOOMING. July to November

HEIGHT. 3 to 5 feet

HABITAT. Full sun to 30% shade

DISTRIBUTION. Uncertain [Hawaii]

INFLORESCENCE.

*Bracts*. 8 to 9; pale orange over most of bract with dark red at base and at tip

*Rachis*. Dark red to maroon proximally and dark red distally, lower bracts dark green proximally

*Sepals*. Light yellow to yellow with distal green band and white or yellow tip, some lighter yellow proximally

*Ovary*. Yellow on top, green on distal half, and yellow below

*Pedicel*. Pale green

VEGETATION. Zingiberoid

*Heliconia hirsuta* L.f. cv. Halloween

BLOOMING. August to December

HEIGHT. 3 to 5 feet

HABITAT. Full sun to 30% shade

DISTRIBUTION. Uncertain [Florida, Hawaii]

INFLORESCENCE.

*Bracts.* 6 to 7; orange, some shading distally to light red; basal bract sometimes with green tip

*Rachis.* Orange, changing to green proximally at inflorescence base

*Sepals.* Orange with green-black distal band and white tip

*Ovary.* Red distally and yellow-orange proximally

*Pedicel.* Orange

VEGETATION. Zingiberoid

*Heliconia hirsuta* L.f. cv. Pancoastal

BLOOMING.    June to November

HEIGHT.    2½ to 8 feet

HABITAT.    Full sun to 40% shade

DISTRIBUTION.    Uncertain [Florida, Brazil]

INFLORESCENCE.

*Bracts.* 6 to 8; red, lighter red on proximal cheek and lip

*Rachis.* Dark red to maroon, sometimes greenish

*Sepals.* Yellow with black distal band and white tip

*Ovary.* Dark green distally, light green below

*Pedicel.* Green

VEGETATION.    Zingiberoid; inflorescence may develop on separate leafless shoot

*Heliconia hirsuta* L.f. cv. Roberto Burle-Marx

BLOOMING. October to March

HEIGHT. 4 to 6 feet

HABITAT. Full sun to 60% shade

DISTRIBUTION. Uncertain [Brazil]

INFLORESCENCE.

*Bracts.* 4 to 6; red, bright red at base

*Rachis.* Maroon on lower bracts and red on upper bracts

*Sepals.* Pale to bright yellow with green-black band distally and whitish tip

*Ovary.* Pale or bright yellow on distal third to half and light green proximally, more yellow on enlarged ovaries

*Pedicel.* Light green

VEGETATION. Zingiberoid

*Heliconia hirsuta* L.f. cv. Trinidad Red

BLOOMING.   All year

HEIGHT.   4 to 8 feet

HABITAT.   Full sun to 30% shade

DISTRIBUTION.   Trinidad [Costa Rica]

INFLORESCENCE.

*Bracts.*  8 to 10; dark red distally shading to orange proximally

*Rachis.*  Orange to yellow, some with pink distally

*Sepals.*  Reddish proximally shading distally to orange to yellow to a green-black band to a dusky white tip

*Ovary.*  Dark green with red top

*Pedicel.*  Light green

VEGETATION.   Zingiberoid

*Heliconia hirsuta* L.f. cv. Twiggy

BLOOMING.   December to March

HEIGHT.   4 to 6 feet

HABITAT.   30% shade

DISTRIBUTION.   Uncertain [Brazil]

INFLORESCENCE.

*Bracts.* 3 to 4; orange at base, pink-red distally, basal bract with green tint

*Rachis.* Yellow, some with green tint

*Sepals.* Orange, pale yellow distally with dark green distal blotch and whitish tip

*Ovary.* Very dark green on distal half, lighter green below

*Pedicel.* Light green

VEGETATION.   Zingiberoid

*Heliconia hirsuta* L.f. cv. Yellow Panama

BLOOMING.   June to September

HEIGHT.   2½ to 7 feet

HABITAT.   Full sun to 20% shade

DISTRIBUTION.   Panama [Florida, Costa Rica]

INFLORESCENCE.

*Bracts.* 5 to 10; yellow with green below the lower bracts

*Rachis.* Yellow

*Sepals.* Yellow with black band distally and white tip

*Ovary.* Dark yellow distally and light yellow below

*Pedicel.* Yellow

VEGETATION.   Zingiberoid

*Heliconia longiflora* R.R. Smith

BLOOMING.   May to January

HEIGHT.   1½ to 15 feet

HABITAT.   Full sun to 50% shade

DISTRIBUTION.   Nicaragua to Colombia [Florida]

INFLORESCENCE.

*Bracts.*  4 to 8; orange

*Rachis.*  Orange

*Sepals.*  White distally and yellow below (an all yellow form occurs in some areas)

*Ovary.*  Orange with green top

*Pedicel.*  Orange

VEGETATION.   Zingiberoid

*Heliconia aurantiaca* Ghiesbreght ex Lemaire

BLOOMING.   December to June

HEIGHT.   1½ to 5 feet

HABITAT.   10 to 40% shade

DISTRIBUTION.   Mexico to Panama [Florida, Hawaii, Barbados]

INFLORESCENCE.

*Bracts.*  3 to 6; orange with pale green tip, turning green with age

*Rachis.*  Orange, turning green

*Sepals.*  Yellow

*Ovary.*  Yellow

*Pedicel.*  Orange

VEGETATION.   Zingiberoid

*Heliconia schiedeana* Klotzsch

BLOOMING. December to August

HEIGHT. 4 to 7 feet

HABITAT. Full sun to 30% shade

DISTRIBUTION. Southern Mexico [California, Florida, Hawaii, Costa Rica]

INFLORESCENCE.

*Bracts.* 7 to 10; red

*Rachis.* Red

*Sepals.* Yellow with green on part of distal half; bent at nearly right angle

*Ovary.* Green distally to lighter green proximally

*Pedicel.* Light green to yellow

VEGETATION. Musoid

*Heliconia spissa* Griggs cv. Guatemala Yellow

BLOOMING.   June to September

HEIGHT.   4 to 12 feet

HABITAT.   Full sun to 30% shade

DISTRIBUTION.   Guatemala [Florida, Costa Rica]

INFLORESCENCE.

*Bracts.* 7 to 13; yellow to red at base, lower bracts with light green along keel and pink tint at base

*Rachis.* Pink to red

*Sepals.* Yellow

*Ovary.* Light green

*Pedicel.* Greenish-yellow

VEGETATION.   Musoid; leaf blades lacerating into lateral segments

*Heliconia spissa* Griggs cv. Mexico Red

BLOOMING.   February to September

HEIGHT.   4 to 8 feet

HABITAT.   Full sun to 30% shade

DISTRIBUTION.   Southern Mexico [Florida, Costa Rica]

INFLORESCENCE.

*Bracts.*  5 to 7; red or pink, lower bracts greenish distally

*Rachis.*  Red or pink

*Sepals.*  Yellow with green tips

*Ovary.*  Green

*Pedicel.*  Yellow-green

VEGETATION.   Musoid; leaf blades lacerating into lateral segments

*Heliconia richardiana* Miquel

BLOOMING. June to November

HEIGHT. 3 to 6 feet

HABITAT. Full sun to 40% shade

DISTRIBUTION. Venezuela through the Guianas to eastern Brazil [Florida, Hawaii, Costa Rica]

INFLORESCENCE.

*Bracts*. 4 to 7; yellow or yellow-green over most of bract with small red or pink-red area at base

*Rachis*. Red or orange

*Sepals*. Light green with yellow flush; bent abruptly backwards near base

*Ovary*. Red

*Pedicel*. Light pink, turning red with elongation

VEGETATION. Musoid

*Heliconia aemygdiana* Burle-Marx ssp.
*aemygdiana*

BLOOMING.    November to
August

HEIGHT.    5 to 12 feet

HABITAT.    Full sun to 60%
shade

DISTRIBUTION.    Amazonian
Colombia to Bolivia and
southeast Brazil [Florida,
Costa Rica]

INFLORESCENCE.

*Bracts.* 3 to 14; rose-pink
over most of bract, yellowish
at base

*Rachis.* Yellow

*Sepals.* Green

*Ovary.* Dark to light green
distally, yellow proximally

*Pedicel.* Yellow to green

VEGETATION.    Musoid

*Heliconia lingulata* Ruiz & Pavón cv. Spiral Fan

BLOOMING.   September to November

HEIGHT.   7 to 9 feet

HABITAT.   Full sun

DISTRIBUTION.   Peru [Florida, Hawaii, Barbados]

INFLORESCENCE.

*Bracts.*  Up to 20; yellow proximally with pink-orange distally, light green on proximal keel and tips

*Rachis.*  Yellow

*Sepals.*  Dull yellow with green tint

*Ovary.*  Green on distal half and yellow proximally

*Pedicel.*  Pale green-yellow

VEGETATION.   Musoid

*Heliconia pseudoaemygdiana* L. Emygdio &
E. Santos cv. Birdiana

BLOOMING.  January to
February and August to
November

HEIGHT.  5 to 13 feet

HABITAT.  Full sun to 30%
shade

DISTRIBUTION.  Brazil,
possibly Ecuador [Florida,
Hawaii, Barbados, Costa
Rica, Venezuela]

INFLORESCENCE.

*Bracts*.  6 to 16; variable,
bracts of some inflores-
cences with yellow prox-
imally and pink-orange distally, others yellow-gold
with orange tips; basal bract
with small green tip

*Rachis*.  Yellow-gold with
some pink between lower
bracts or pink-orange and
yellow above

*Sepals*.  Green-yellow distally
and pale yellow-green or
yellow proximally

*Ovary*.  Light green, turning
darker with age

*Pedicel*.  Light green

VEGETATION.  Musoid

*Heliconia latispatha* Bentham cv. Distans

BLOOMING.  All year, peak April to September

HEIGHT.   1½ to 5½ feet

HABITAT.   Full sun to 40% shade

DISTRIBUTION.   Uncertain [Florida, Hawaii, Barbados, Venezuela]

INFLORESCENCE.

*Bracts.* 3 to 7; usually red on distal half and yellow or golden proximally, some with green on cheeks; basal bract with green keel and usually with green leaflet; second and third bracts often with green keel and tip

*Rachis.* Usually yellow, some with green tint or golden

*Sepals.* Pale yellow-green, with dark green stripe along distal margin and at base

*Ovary.* Light green distally and pale yellow below

*Pedicel.* Pale yellow

VEGETATION.   Musoid; older leaves usually with thin maroon margin

*Heliconia latispatha* Bentham cv. Red-Yellow Gyro

BLOOMING.    All year with peak May to September

HEIGHT.    5 to 18 feet

HABITAT.    Full sun to 50% shade

DISTRIBUTION.    Mexico to South America [widely cultivated]

INFLORESCENCE.

*Bracts.* 6 to 18; usually red over most of bract with small area of yellow or gold at base; basal bract with green keel and usually with green leaflet

*Rachis.* Usually yellow with faint green tint, some golden

*Sepals.* Pale yellow-green, usually with dark green stripe along margins most of length

*Ovary.* Green distally and pale yellow proximally

*Pedicel.* Pale yellow

VEGETATION.    Musoid; usually with very thin maroon margin along leaves, rarely with maroon lower midrib

*Heliconia latispatha* Bentham cv. Orange Gyro

BLOOMING.    All year with peak June to August

HEIGHT.    5 to 16 feet

HABITAT.    Full sun to 50% shade

DISTRIBUTION.    Mexico to South America [widely cultivated]

INFLORESCENCE.

*Bracts.* 7 to 17; usually orange over most of bract, basal bract with green keel and usually with green terminal leaflet; next several bracts upward with green distal keel and tip

*Rachis.* Usually yellow with green tint

*Sepals.* Pale yellow-green, with dark green stripe along margins for most of length

*Ovary.* Cream, usually with pale green distally

*Pedicel.* Cream

VEGETATION.    Musoid; usually with a very thin maroon margin along leaves, rarely with maroon lower midrib

*Heliconia sarapiquensis* Daniels & Stiles

BLOOMING. July to November

HEIGHT. 4 to 9 feet

HABITAT. 20 to 50% shade

DISTRIBUTION. Costa Rica [Florida]

INFLORESCENCE.

*Bracts.* 8 to 10; red

*Rachis.* Bright yellow, extending slightly onto bract base

*Sepals.* Bright yellow distally, becoming paler below

*Ovary.* Pale yellow

*Pedicel.* Pale yellow

VEGETATION. Musoid; lower surface with reddish blotches on midrib

*Heliconia lindsayana* Kress

BLOOMING.  May to August

HEIGHT.  4 to 8 feet

HABITAT.  Full sun to 40% shade

DISTRIBUTION.  Panama [Florida, Hawaii, Costa Rica]

INFLORESCENCE.

*Bracts*.  7 to 11; red (sometimes pink)
*Rachis*.  Yellow (sometimes pink)

*Sepals*.  Yellow or yellow with green tint
*Ovary*.  Cream with green tint near top or pale green
*Pedicel*.  Cream

VEGETATION.  Musoid; lower surface with maroon midrib with color extending onto petiole, blades sometimes with white waxy coating below

*Heliconia lutea* Kress

BLOOMING.   June to October

HEIGHT.   4 to 7 feet

HABITAT.   Full sun to 50% shade

DISTRIBUTION.   Panama [Hawaii]

INFLORESCENCE.

*Bracts.*  5 to 7; yellow-green

*Rachis.* Light yellow-green with bright yellow spots near bract

*Sepals.* Yellow to green distally

*Ovary.* Pale yellow

*Pedicel.* Pale yellow

VEGETATION.   Musoid

*Heliconia thomasiana* Kress

BLOOMING.    September to March

HEIGHT.    3 to 5 feet

HABITAT.    Full sun to 50% shade

DISTRIBUTION.    Panama [Florida, Hawaii, Brazil, Costa Rica, Venezuela]

INFLORESCENCE.

*Bracts.* 3 to 7; variable, all with red base, yellow or yellow-green over most of bract with green keel and tip

*Rachis.* Red to yellow

*Sepals.* Green distally and white-green or yellowish proximally

*Ovary.* White

*Pedicel.* White

VEGETATION.    Musoid

*Heliconia beckneri* R.R. Smith cv. Hall Red

BLOOMING. December to July

HEIGHT. 6 to 9 feet

HABITAT. 40% shade

DISTRIBUTION. Costa Rica [Florida]

INFLORESCENCE.

*Bracts.* 7 to 10; red, basal bract with green-yellow keel and tip

*Rachis.* Red

*Sepals.* Pale green shading to darker green at tip

*Ovary.* Pale green

*Pedicel.* Pale green

VEGETATION. Musoid

*Heliconia beckneri* R.R. Smith cv. Yellow Gyre

BLOOMING. All year with peak June to August

HEIGHT. 7 to 15 feet

HABITAT. 30 to 60% shade

DISTRIBUTION. Costa Rica [Florida, Hawaii]

INFLORESCENCE.

*Bracts.* 8 to 12; yellow, basal and sometimes other bracts with green tint along keel, lower bracts rarely with scarlet blotches along keel

*Rachis.* Solid green, or yellow on bract side and green on opposite side

*Sepals.* Dark green distally to white proximally

*Ovary.* Greenish distally and cream proximally

*Pedicel.* Cream

VEGETATION. Musoid

*Heliconia irrasa* R.R. Smith ssp. *irrasa*

BLOOMING.  May to September

HEIGHT.  3 to 6 feet

HABITAT.  10 to 50% shade

DISTRIBUTION.  Costa Rica and Panama [Florida]

INFLORESCENCE.

*Bracts.*  4 to 9; variable, solid red, orange or yellow proximally and red distally, or red with thin gold-yellow lip; basal bract usually with green keel and tip

*Rachis.*  Usually yellow, some with green, red, or maroon

*Sepals.*  Gold or yellow distally and pale yellow proximally

*Ovary.*  Light yellow

*Pedicel.*  Yellow

VEGETATION.  Musoid; some with contrasting white midrib on upper surface

*Heliconia irrasa* ssp. *undulata* Daniels & Stiles

BLOOMING.    May to September

HEIGHT.    2½ to 6 feet

HABITAT.    30 to 50% shade

DISTRIBUTION.    Costa Rica [Florida]

INFLORESCENCE.

*Bracts.*  5 to 11; variable, primarily red, sometimes with yellow cheek; basal bract with green keel and tip

*Rachis.*  Solid red or red and yellow

*Sepals.*  Yellow, often gold at distal end

*Ovary.*  Pale yellow

*Pedicel.*  Pale yellow

VEGETATION.    Musoid; some forms with upper leaf surface dark lustrous green with pale midrib

*Heliconia spathocircinata* Aristeguieta

BLOOMING.  May to September

HEIGHT.  3 to 7 feet

HABITAT.  Full sun to 40% shade

DISTRIBUTION.  Tropical South America [widely cultivated]

INFLORESCENCE.

*Bracts*.  6 to 12; variously red, green, and yellow, e.g., green with red lip, or lower cheek and keel yellowish-green with upper cheek and lip red or orange, or all yellow

*Rachis*.  Green, red, or yellow

*Sepals*.  Yellow

*Ovary*.  Light green

*Pedicel*.  Pale yellow

VEGETATION.  Musoid

*Heliconia tortuosa* Griggs cv. Red Twist

BLOOMING.    February to November

HEIGHT.    5 to 10 feet

HABITAT.    Full sun to 70% shade

DISTRIBUTION.    Costa Rica [Florida, Hawaii, Barbados, Brazil]

INFLORESCENCE.

*Bracts.* 6 to 10; red, some-times with yellow at base of bracts; basal bract with green keel and tip

*Rachis.* Red, some with yellow

*Sepals.* Yellow

*Ovary.* Green

*Pedicel.* Green

VEGETATION.    Musoid; lower midrib sometimes maroon

*Heliconia tortuosa* Griggs cv. Yellow Twist

BLOOMING.   June to January

HEIGHT.   9 to 12 feet

HABITAT.   30 to 60% shade

DISTRIBUTION.   Costa Rica [Florida]

INFLORESCENCE.

*Bracts*.  5 to 12; yellow with pale green keel and tip, some with green-yellow or yellow with red lips and tips

*Rachis*.  Pale green

*Sepals*.  Yellow with pale green tip

*Ovary*.  Green, darker on distal half

*Pedicel*.  Green

VEGETATION.   Musoid

*Heliconia monteverdensis* Daniels & Stiles

BLOOMING.   March to July, sometimes into November

HEIGHT.   3 to 6 feet

HABITAT.   20 to 70% shade

DISTRIBUTION.   Costa Rica [Florida, Hawaii]

INFLORESCENCE.

*Bracts.* 5 to 9; dark red, slightly maroon along keel

*Rachis.* Red to dark red

*Sepals.* White, cream, or pale yellow with green tint

*Ovary.* Light green on distal half and pale yellow proximally

*Pedicel.* Light green or white

VEGETATION.   Musoid; usually with maroon on stem, petiole, and lower midrib, sometimes lower midrib with red or maroon blotching

*Heliconia umbrophila* Daniels & Stiles

BLOOMING.    June to October

HEIGHT.    4 to 8 feet

HABITAT.    40 to 80% shade

DISTRIBUTION.    Costa Rica [Florida, Hawaii, Barbados]

INFLORESCENCE.

*Bracts.* 5 to 8; dull yellow, or yellow with green tint

*Rachis.* Pale yellow, or yellow with green tint

*Sepals.* Creamy white shading to light yellow distally

*Ovary.* Pale yellow

*Pedicel.* White

VEGETATION.    Musoid; lower leaf surface with dark purple or maroon, particularly in young leaves; midrib light green to maroon, changing with age

*Heliconia paka* A.C. Smith

BLOOMING. August to February

HEIGHT. 6 to 15 feet

HABITAT. Full sun to 50% shade

DISTRIBUTION. Fiji [Hawaii]

INFLORESCENCE.

*Bracts.* 12 to 16; green, sometimes yellow inside

*Rachis.* Green

*Sepals.* Yellow becoming green at tip

*Ovary.* Yellow; mature fruits yellow-orange

*Pedicel.* Light green

VEGETATION. Musoid

*Heliconia laufao* Kress

BLOOMING.   Throughout the year

HEIGHT.   12 to 20 feet

HABITAT.   Full sun to 50% shade

DISTRIBUTION.   American and Western Samoa [Hawaii]

INFLORESCENCE.

*Bracts.*  10 to 20; green outside with yellow along margins and at rachis, yellow to reddish within

*Rachis.*  Hidden, green

*Sepals.*  Yellow-orange

*Ovary.*  Yellow to orange; mature fruits deep red

*Pedicel.*  Yellow

VEGETATION.   Musoid

*Heliconia mariae* J.D. Hooker

BLOOMING.  All year

HEIGHT.  15 to 23 feet

HABITAT.  Full sun to 50% shade

DISTRIBUTION.  Guatemala to Colombia [widely cultivated]

INFLORESCENCE.

*Bracts.*  40 to 65; red

*Rachis.*  Red to yellow

*Sepals.*  Rose red at tip, clear white at base

*Ovary.*  White

*Pedicel.*  White to pink

VEGETATION.  Musoid; maroon tint along lower leaf midrib

*Heliconia mariae* J.D. Hooker × *H. pogonantha* var. *holerythra* Daniels & Stiles cv. Bushmaster

BLOOMING.    All year

HEIGHT.    15 to 20 feet

HABITAT.    Full sun to 50% shade

DISTRIBUTION.    Costa Rica [Florida]

INFLORESCENCE.

*Bracts.*  40 to 60; red

*Rachis.*  Red

*Sepals.*  Faint yellow at tip, mostly clear white, and faint pink at base

*Ovary.*  White

*Pedicel.*  White

VEGETATION.    Musoid; maroon tint near petiole of lower leaf midrib

*Heliconia rostrata* Ruiz & Pavón

BLOOMING.  All year

HEIGHT.  3 to 20 feet

HABITAT.  Full sun to 50% shade

DISTRIBUTION.  Originally from Amazonian Peru and Ecuador, now widely cultivated around the world

INFLORESCENCE.

*Bracts.*  4 to 35; red over most of bract to yellow, green-yellow distally, lip yellow-green proximally to green distally

*Rachis.*  Red

*Sepals.*  Bright yellow distally turning lighter to almost clear-white at base

*Ovary.*  White

*Pedicel.*  White

VEGETATION.  Musoid; lower leaf midrib with bright or dark stripe from slightly above axil onto petiole, absent on some, leaf blades lacerating into lateral segments

*sometimes spiral

*Heliconia mutisiana* Cuatrecasas

BLOOMING. June to November

HEIGHT. 7 to 22 feet

HABITAT. Full sun to 50% shade

DISTRIBUTION. Colombia [Florida, Hawaii, Puerto Rico]

INFLORESCENCE.

*Bracts.* 10 to 26; red to pink, upper bracts with yellow ex-tending onto cheek at base; basal bract with green on distal cheek; bracts covered with buff hairs

*Rachis.* Pink and yellow

*Sepals.* Pale yellow with green tint distally, clear at base

*Ovary.* Cream

*Pedicel.* Cream

VEGETATION. Musoid

*Heliconia dielsiana* Loesener

BLOOMING.  January to July

HEIGHT.  9 to 13 feet

HABITAT.  Full sun to 50% shade

DISTRIBUTION.  Colombia and Ecuador [Costa Rica]

INFLORESCENCE.

*Bracts.*  10 to 25; orange-red to red, lower bracts very green at tip on some

*Rachis.*  Red

*Sepals.*  Yellow

*Ovary.*  Pale yellow

*Pedicel.*  Pale yellow

VEGETATION.  Musoid; some with purplish-tint on lower midrib

*Heliconia solomonensis* Kress

BLOOMING.  July to March

HEIGHT.  15 to 22 feet

HABITAT.  Full sun to 50% shade

DISTRIBUTION.  Solomon Islands and Papua New Guinea [Hawaii, Costa Rica]

INFLORESCENCE.

*Bracts*.  10 to 18; green, yellow at base on some

*Rachis*.  Green to yellow

*Sepals*.  Green at tip and white proximally

*Ovary*.  Lemon yellow; mature fruits bright orange

*Pedicel*.  White

VEGETATION.  Musoid

*Heliconia stilesii* Kress

BLOOMING. All year, mainly June to September

HEIGHT. 12 to 26 feet

HABITAT. Full sun to 50% shade

DISTRIBUTION. Costa Rica [Florida]

INFLORESCENCE.

*Bracts.* 20 to 35; red

*Rachis.* Red

*Sepals.* Gold on distal half shading to yellow or cream

*Ovary.* Cream

*Pedicel.* Cream

VEGETATION. Musoid; white waxy coating on lower leaf surface, lower midrib yellow-green with maroon overstripe

*Heliconia longa* (Griggs) Winkler

BLOOMING.   All year with peak in July to September

HEIGHT.   12 to 25 feet

HABITAT.   Full sun to 50% shade

DISTRIBUTION.   Nicaragua to Ecuador [Florida, Hawaii]

INFLORESCENCE.

*Bracts.* 11 to 60; red, some shading near rachis to yellow-orange

*Rachis.* Red, red-orange, or red-and-cream

*Sepals.* Gold or yellow distally, yellow, light pink, or white proximally

*Ovary.* White or cream

*Pedicel.* White or cream

VEGETATION.   Musoid; white waxy coating covering lower surface of leaf blade (denser with less shade); lower midrib on some yellow, pink, or red-green

*Heliconia standleyi* Macbride

BLOOMING. June to March

HEIGHT. 13 to 26 feet

HABITAT. Full sun to 50% shade, often in standing water

DISTRIBUTION. Southern Colombia to northern Peru [Florida, Hawaii, Australia, Brazil]

INFLORESCENCE.

*Bracts.* 20 to 55; red over most of bract to green or green-yellow on distal end
*Rachis.* Red
*Sepals.* Green on distal half to white proximally
*Ovary.* White
*Pedicel.* White

VEGETATION. Musoid

*Heliconia nigripraefixa* Dodson & Gentry

BLOOMING.  September to March

HEIGHT.  10 to 20 feet

HABITAT.  Full sun to 30% shade

DISTRIBUTION.  Colombia and Ecuador [Florida, Costa Rica]

INFLORESCENCE.

*Bracts.*  25 to 35; red to red-orange, tip black becoming necrotic with age

*Rachis.*  Red to red-orange

*Sepals.*  Yellow on distal third, white proximally

*Ovary.*  White to pale lavender

*Pedicel.*  White

VEGETATION.  Musoid; leaf blades lacerating into lateral segments

*Heliconia pastazae* L. Anderss.

BLOOMING.   May to November

HEIGHT.   12 to 15 feet

HABITAT.   Full sun to 30% shade

DISTRIBUTION.   Ecuador [Hawaii]

INFLORESCENCE.

*Bracts.*  19 to 30; red with narrow yellow lip

*Rachis.*  Red or maroon, yellow near younger bracts

*Sepals.*  Yellow distally to white proximally

*Ovary.*  White

*Pedicel.*  White

VEGETATION.   Musoid

*Heliconia pogonantha* var. *holerythra*
Daniels & Stiles

BLOOMING.   All year with peak January and February

HEIGHT.   10 to 25 feet

HABITAT.   20 to 40% shade

DISTRIBUTION.   Costa Rica and Panama [Florida]

INFLORESCENCE.

*Bracts.* 15 to 40; red, some pink at base and some with cream area on proximal lip; lip and tip becoming black (necrotic) with age

*Rachis.* Red, some pink or pink-cream

*Sepals.* Yellow on distal half and pale cream, white, or pink proximally

*Ovary.* White or cream

*Pedicel.* White or cream

VEGETATION.   Musoid

*Heliconia pogonantha* Cufodontis var. *pogonantha*

BLOOMING.   All year, primarily January to August

HEIGHT.   12 to 25 feet

HABITAT.   20 to 50% shade

DISTRIBUTION.   Costa Rica and Nicaragua [Florida]

INFLORESCENCE.

*Bracts.* 10 to 50; red over most of bract with yellow at base near rachis (variations between clumps on relative amount of red and yellow); lip becoming necrotic with age

*Rachis.* Yellow

*Sepals.* Pale yellow distally and cream proximally

*Ovary.* Cream

*Pedicel.* Cream

VEGETATION.   Musoid

*Heliconia vellerigera* Poeppig

BLOOMING.   All year

HEIGHT.   15 to 20 feet

HABITAT.   Full sun to 50% shade

DISTRIBUTION.   Colombia, Ecuador, and Peru [Florida, Hawaii, Costa Rica]

INFLORESCENCE.

*Bracts.*  20 to 30; red, very "wooly" with cinnamon hairs

*Rachis.*  Red with wooly hairs

*Sepals.*  Deep yellow on distal ⅔ and paler proximally

*Ovary.*  White

*Pedicel.*  Light yellow

VEGETATION.   Musoid

*Heliconia danielsiana* Kress

BLOOMING.  All year with peak June to August

HEIGHT.  10 to 24 feet

HABITAT.  Full sun to 60% shade

DISTRIBUTION.  Costa Rica [Florida]

INFLORESCENCE.

*Bracts.* 20 to 30; crimson to orange-red, bracts very hirsute or "wooly"

*Rachis.* Pale orange-red

*Sepals.* Deep yellow on distal ⅔, paler proximally with yellow hairs

*Ovary.* Cream

*Pedicel.* Cream

VEGETATION.  Musoid; thin waxy coating on lower leaf surface, but lacking on some, lower midrib sometimes maroon

*Heliconia magnifica* Kress

BLOOMING.   All year, mainly March to September

HEIGHT.   7 to 18 feet

HABITAT.   20 to 60% shade

DISTRIBUTION.   Panama [Florida, Costa Rica]

INFLORESCENCE.

*Bracts.* 16 to 35; dark red on proximal cheek, shading to burgundy distally, maroon on lip; lip becoming necrotic with age, progressing from basal bract downward; bracts very hirsute or "wooly"

*Rachis.* Red to burgundy, often dark red between proximal bracts, becoming light red to cream-red between distal bracts

*Sepals.* Yellow on distal half and clear-white proximally

*Ovary.* White

*Pedicel.* White; sometimes pink near ovary

VEGETATION.   Musoid; maroon margin on lower surface of some leaves

*Heliconia ramonensis* Daniels & Stiles
var. *ramonensis*

BLOOMING.    Possibly all year with peak April to July
HEIGHT.    8 to 15 feet
HABITAT.    20 to 60% shade
DISTRIBUTION.    Costa Rica and Panama [Florida, Hawaii]

INFLORESCENCE.

*Bracts.* 15 to 40; variable, red, rose-red, or pink, usually pink-red proximally, shading to dark red distally
*Rachis.* Usually reddish at basal bract, changing to cream and pink between distal bracts, yellowish on some
*Sepals.* Usually yellow on distal ⅔ and clear-white proximally
*Ovary.* White
*Pedicel.* White

VEGETATION.    Musoid; leaf color variable, usually lower surface almost all maroon with midrib either yellow-green or with maroon stripe on each side; some leaves on some plants with little or no maroon color

*Heliconia xanthovillosa* Kress

BLOOMING.   May to October

HEIGHT.   10 to 20 feet

HABITAT.   Full sun to 50% shade

DISTRIBUTION.   Panama [Florida, Costa Rica]

INFLORESCENCE.

*Bracts.* Bright yellow to yellow-green, with yellow "wooly" hairs

*Rachis.* Bright yellow with yellow hairs

*Sepals.* White basally to yellow at tip

*Ovary.* White

*Pedicel.* White

VEGETATION.   Musoid

*Heliconia pendula* Wawra cv. Bright Red

BLOOMING.  April to July

HEIGHT.  5 to 9 feet

HABITAT.  20 to 40% shade

DISTRIBUTION.  Northern South America [Florida, Hawaii, Costa Rica]

INFLORESCENCE.

*Bracts.* 4 to 9; bright red

*Rachis.* Red
*Sepals.* White
*Ovary.* Pale yellow
*Pedicel.* Pale yellow

VEGETATION.  Musoid; maroon on newer stems, no white waxy coating

*Heliconia pendula* Wawra cv. Frosty

BLOOMING.   July to November

HEIGHT.   6 to 12 feet

HABITAT.   20 to 50% shade

DISTRIBUTION.   Uncertain [Hawaii]

INFLORESCENCE.

*Bracts.* 8 to 10; pink-red on basal part of bract and onto keel, with yellow-white on distal cheek, lip, and tip (more yellow on younger bracts)

*Rachis.* Red or deep red

*Sepals.* White

*Ovary.* White with yellow tint

*Pedicel.* White with yellow tint

VEGETATION.   Musoid; white waxy coating on stem, petiole, and lower leaf surface

*Heliconia pendula* Wawra cv. Red Waxy

BLOOMING.  April to September

HEIGHT.  4 to 16 feet

HABITAT.  Full sun to 40% shade

DISTRIBUTION.  Guyana [widely cultivated]

INFLORESCENCE.

*Bracts.*  5 to 11; dull red or pink

*Rachis.*  Pink
*Sepals.*  White
*Ovary.*  White
*Pedicel.*  White

VEGETATION.  Musoid; white waxy coating on stem, petiole, and lower leaf surface (rarely absent)

*Heliconia nutans* Woodson

BLOOMING.    February to September with peak June and July

HEIGHT.    3 to 7 feet

HABITAT.    Full sun to 30% shade

DISTRIBUTION.    Costa Rica and Panama [Florida, Hawaii]

INFLORESCENCE.

*Bracts.* 3 to 12; light to dark red, often with flush of orange-red on cheek near proximal lip; basal bract on some with green distal keel and leaflet, some with green on second and third bracts

*Rachis.* Red to orange-red, yellow on some

*Sepals.* Yellow, some gold near tip

*Ovary.* Yellow or light green

*Pedicel.* Cream-yellow

VEGETATION.    Musoid; on some, maroon on lower surface of blade and midrib

*Heliconia chartacea* Lane ex Barreiros
cv. Sexy Pink

BLOOMING.   All year

HEIGHT.   6 to 16 feet

HABITAT.   Full sun to 50% shade

DISTRIBUTION.   Guianas to Amazon Basin [Florida, Hawaii, Barbados, Costa Rica]

INFLORESCENCE.

*Bracts.* 4 to 28; carmine at base and on proximal ⅔ of cheek and keel, a narrow pale stripe subtends thicker pale to dark green lip and tip

*Rachis.* Mandarin red

*Sepals.* Dark green distally to paler green proximally

*Ovary.* Cream

*Pedicel.* Cream

VEGETATION.   Musoid; moderate white waxy coating on most stems, older leaf blades lacerating into narrow lateral segments

*Heliconia chartacea* Lane ex Barreiros
cv. Sexy Scarlet

BLOOMING.   November to
August

HEIGHT.   5 to 14 feet

HABITAT.   Full sun to 40%
shade

DISTRIBUTION.   Guianas
and Brazil [Hawaii, Costa
Rica]

INFLORESCENCE.

*Bracts.* 4 to 13; scarlet along
base and most of cheek, pale
to dark green along lip and
on tip; basal bract mostly
green

*Rachis.* Scarlet

*Sepals.* Dark green distally
to light green proximally, often clear at base

*Ovary.* Cream

*Pedicel.* Cream

VEGETATION.   Musoid;
white waxy coating on
stems, leaves, and often on
bracts; most older leaf blades
lacerating into narrow
lateral segments

*Heliconia platystachys* Baker

BLOOMING. February to October with peak July to September

HEIGHT. 12 to 18 feet

HABITAT. Full sun to 40% shade

DISTRIBUTION. Costa Rica to Colombia [widely cultivated]

INFLORESCENCE.

*Bracts.* 10 to 20; red on cheek, proximal lip, and keel to yellow with green tint proximally

*Rachis.* Red, changing to yellow near younger bracts on some

*Sepals.* Yellow to gold, shading to cream-yellow or yellow-green proximally

*Ovary.* Cream, changing to pale yellow with age

*Pedicel.* Pale yellow or cream

VEGETATION. Musoid; white waxy coating usual on stem, petiole, and lower midrib, also waxy on lower leaf blade on some

*Heliconia collinsiana* Griggs var. *collinsiana*

BLOOMING.    All year with peak January to September

HEIGHT.    5 to 16 feet

HABITAT.    Full sun to 50% shade

DISTRIBUTION.    Southern Mexico to central Nicaragua [widely cultivated]

INFLORESCENCE.

*Bracts.* 6 to 14; dark red to orange-red, younger bracts with yellow at base and on proximal lip; basal bract on some with green keel and tip

*Rachis.* Red at large upper bracts, changing to red-yellow or yellow at small lower bracts

*Sepals.* Yellow to orange-yellow or gold

*Ovary.* Yellow

*Pedicel.* Yellow to pale gold, some with pink tint at base

VEGETATION.    Musoid; white waxy coating on shoot, lower blade, and irregularly on bracts; maroon stripe or blotch on lower midrib extending out from axil of most leaves

*Heliconia secunda* R.R. Smith

BLOOMING.    February to August with peak May and June

HEIGHT.    4 to 14 feet

HABITAT.    30 to 60% shade

DISTRIBUTION.    Costa Rica and Nicaragua [Florida]

INFLORESCENCE.

*Bracts.* 8 to 18; dark red to scarlet; basal bract with mottled green on keel

*Rachis.* Dark red or red

*Sepals.* Yellow or pale yellow on distal third and cream or white proximally

*Ovary.* Pale green

*Pedicel.* Pale yellow or white or cream

VEGETATION.    Musoid; some with mottled dark red or maroon on upper stem

*some contorted

*Heliconia secunda* R.R. Smith × *H. clinophila* R.R. Smith
cv. Toucan

BLOOMING.   May to
August

HEIGHT.   4 to 6 feet

HABITAT.   Full sun to 40%
shade

DISTRIBUTION.   Costa Rica

INFLORESCENCE.

*Bracts.* 3 to 7; red (revoluted
lips expose inner bract surface of red and light green-

yellow); basal bract with
green cheek and keel and
dark red lip

*Rachis.* Light yellow or red

*Sepals.* Light yellow with
green tint on distal ⅔

*Ovary.* Pale green

*Pedicel.* Light yellow

VEGETATION.   Musoid; up-
per surface with raised veins

*or contorted

*Heliconia marginata* (Griggs) Pittier

BLOOMING.   All year with peak in June and July

HEIGHT.   5 to 15 feet

HABITAT.   Full sun to 30% shade, often in standing water

DISTRIBUTION.   Costa Rica to Peru [Florida, Hawaii, Barbados, Brazil]

INFLORESCENCE.

*Bracts*.  5 to 15; red with yellow lip and tip

*Rachis*.  Red, some with small yellow area

*Sepals*.  Bright yellow, orange, or pale yellow

*Ovary*.  Yellow or yellowish-cream

*Pedicel*.  Yellow or cream with proximal pink tint

VEGETATION.   Musoid; leaves held stiffly erect

*Heliconia* × *rauliniana* Barreiros (*H. marginata* × *H. bihai*)

BLOOMING.   September to April

HEIGHT.   10 to 15 feet

HABITAT.   Full sun to 80% shade

DISTRIBUTION.   Uncertain [Florida, Hawaii, Brazil, Venezuela]

*some erect
**contorted or serpentine

INFLORESCENCE.

*Bracts.*  10 to 15; red with yellow-green on distal lip to tip
*Rachis.*  Dark red
*Sepals.*  Green on all or part of distal half and white proximally (some with proximal yellow tint)
*Ovary.*  White
*Pedicel.*  White
VEGETATION.   Musoid

*Heliconia griggsiana* L.B. Smith cv. Angry Moon

BLOOMING. September to March

HEIGHT. 6 to 29 feet

HABITAT. Full sun to 40% shade

DISTRIBUTION. Western Ecuador [Brazil, Costa Rica, Venezuela]

INFLORESCENCE.

*Bracts.* 9 to 30; red at base, or pink and then red, pale red along lip, dark red on tip (with green tip on first two bracts), dark gray-blue-green, sometimes blackish-purple, on most of cheek and keel

*Rachis.* Pink or red, rarely yellowish

*Sepals.* Gold distally to yellow proximally

*Ovary.* Yellow-cream

*Pedicel.* Yellow-cream

VEGETATION. Musoid; white waxy coating mainly on younger shoots, on petiole, and on lower blade; maroon upper and lower midrib, extending as maroon blotches onto petiole

*Heliconia griggsiana* L.B. Smith cv. Blue Moon

BLOOMING. September to November

HEIGHT. 6 to 28 feet

HABITAT. Full sun to 40% shade

DISTRIBUTION. Northern Ecuador and Colombia [Costa Rica]

INFLORESCENCE.

*Bracts.* 5 to 30; green over cheek and keel, yellow at base and along lip (also on tip of lower bracts); basal bract mostly green

*Rachis.* Cream with yellow tint

*Sepals.* Gold distally to yellow proximally

*Ovary.* Yellow-cream

*Pedicel.* Yellow-cream

VEGETATION. Musoid; white waxy coating on newer shoots, petiole, and lower surface of leaf blade; pale maroon stripe on lower midrib

*Heliconia curtispatha* Petersen

BLOOMING.    August to March

HEIGHT.    15 to 21 feet

HABITAT.    Full sun to 30% shade

DISTRIBUTION.    Panama and Colombia [Brazil, Costa Rica]

INFLORESCENCE.

*Bracts.* 21 to 30; red, some inflorescences with bracts light red proximally and shading to dark red distally, especially along lip; lip margin and tip becoming necrotic with age

*Rachis.* Red, sometimes yellow near younger distal bracts

*Sepals.* Gold or deep yellow on distal third, shading to yellow to clear proximally

*Ovary.* White

*Pedicel.* White

VEGETATION.    Musoid; lower midrib yellow-white with median maroon stripe on some

*or nodding

*Heliconia trichocarpa* Daniels & Stiles

BLOOMING.   July to November, peaking September and October

HEIGHT.   6 to 12 feet

HABITAT.   30 to 70% shade

DISTRIBUTION.   Costa Rica to Colombia [Florida, Hawaii]

INFLORESCENCE.

*Bracts.*  6 to 10; Red to rose-red, basal bract with green infusion; tips becoming necrotic with age

*Rachis.* Red

*Sepals.* Yellow, fading to pale white near base

*Ovary.* Pale white to pale yellow (or pink)

*Pedicel.* Pale cream

VEGETATION.   Musoid

*Heliconia colgantea* R.R. Smith ex Daniels & Stiles

BLOOMING. January to November with peak July to August

HEIGHT. 6 to 14 feet

HABITAT. 30 to 60% shade

DISTRIBUTION. Costa Rica and Panama [Hawaii, Barbados, Brazil]

INFLORESCENCE.

*Bracts.* 7 to 11; pink over most of upper bracts with flush of cream at base and onto lip, basal bracts with green tips

*Rachis.* Pink-red to light pink on some, darker red on others

*Sepals.* Dark yellow distally to yellow proximally

*Ovary.* Light yellow or cream

*Pedicel.* Light yellow or cream

VEGETATION. Musoid

*Heliconia talamancana* Daniels & Stiles

BLOOMING. June to November

HEIGHT. 6 to 15 feet

HABITAT. 30 to 60% shade

DISTRIBUTION. Costa Rica and Panama [Florida]

INFLORESCENCE.

*Bracts.* 6 to 13; green over most of bract, shading darker distally, some with red at base

*Rachis.* Red to maroon, some with green and red

*Sepals.* Green tinted distally to clear yellow proximally

*Ovary.* White

*Pedicel.* White

VEGETATION. Musoid

*Heliconia necrobracteata* Kress

BLOOMING. April to August

HEIGHT. 10 to 15 feet

HABITAT. 50% shade

DISTRIBUTION. Panama [Hawaii, Costa Rica]

INFLORESCENCE.

*Bracts*. 10 to 20; red, tips becoming black and necrotic
*Rachis*. Red
*Sepals*. Yellow
*Ovary*. Pale yellow
*Pedicel*. Pale yellow

VEGETATION. Musoid

*Heliconia lanata* (Green) Kress

BLOOMING.   All year

HEIGHT.   10 to 15 feet

HABITAT.   30 to 50% shade

DISTRIBUTION.   Solomon Islands [Hawaii, Costa Rica]

INFLORESCENCE.

*Bracts*.  10 to 20; light green over most of bract, orange at base

*Rachis*.  Orange

*Sepals*.  White or yellow with green at tip

*Ovary*.  Yellow to orange; mature fruits orange

*Pedicel*.  White

VEGETATION.   Musoid

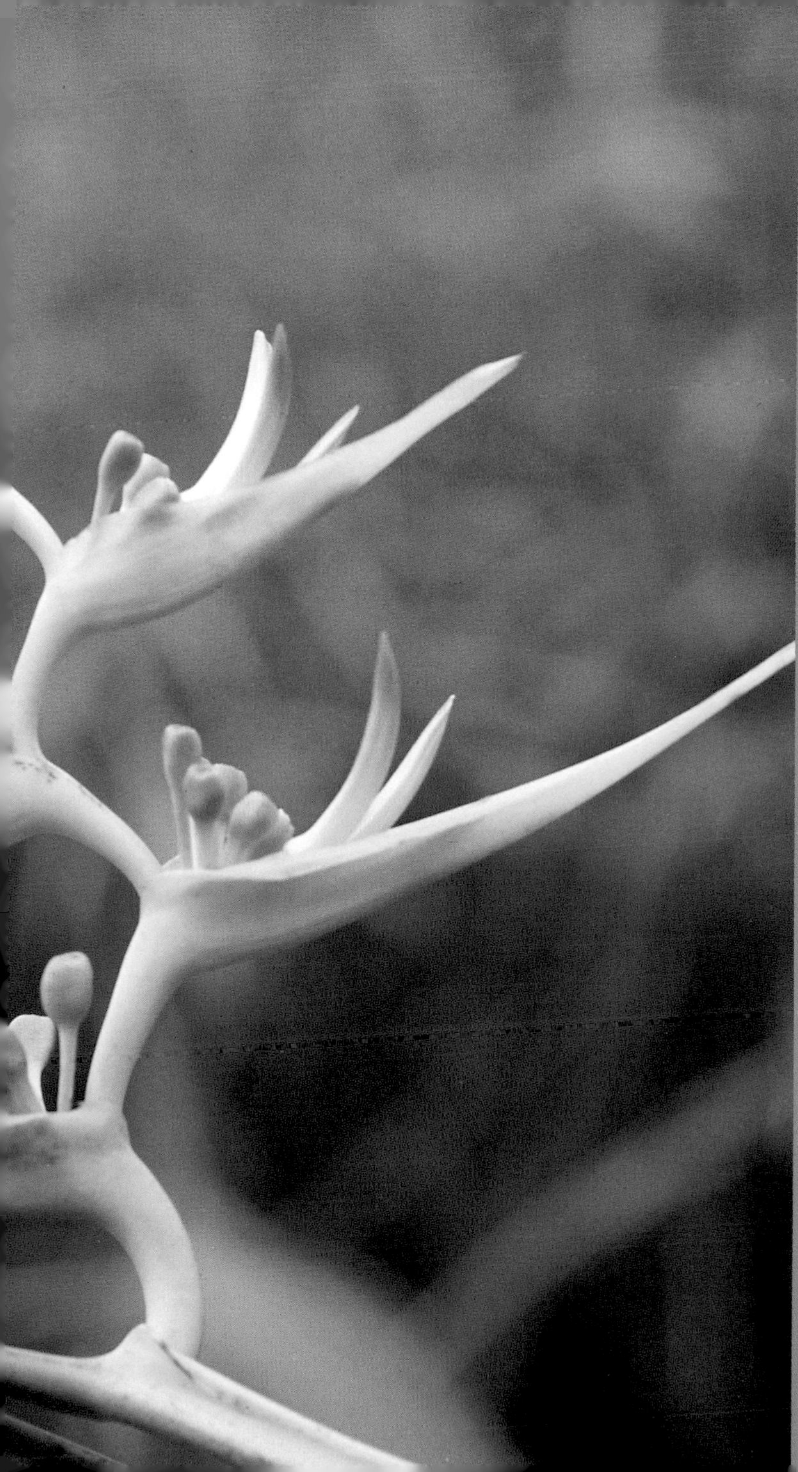

RESOURCES

# Where to See Heliconias

No book or photograph can adequately portray or allow a full appreciation of the color and form of heliconias. At best one should see them in their native tropical habitats. When this is not possible, botanical gardens provide a proper setting to view heliconias. Listed below are several gardens that maintain or are building outstanding collections of species and cultivars of *Heliconia*, the majority of which are included in this guide. We highly recommend that readers visit these gardens.

*Andromeda Gardens
Bathsheba
St. Joseph, Barbados

*Flamingo Gardens
3750 Flamingo Road
Ft. Lauderdale, Florida 33330
U.S.A.

*Jurong BirdPark
Jurong Hill
Jalan Ahmad Ibrahim
Singapore 2262

*Harold L. Lyon Arboretum
University of Honolulu
3860 Manoa Road
Honolulu, Hawaii 96820
U.S.A.

*National Tropical Botanical
    Garden
P.O. Box 340
Lawai, Kauai, Hawaii 96765
U.S.A.

United States Botanic Garden
Washington, D.C. 20024
U.S.A.

Waimea Arboretum and
   Botanical Garden
59-864 Kamehameha Highway
Haleiwa, Hawaii 96712
U.S.A.

*Jardín Botánico Robert y
   Catherine Wilson
Apartado 35
San Vito de Java, Coto Brus
Costa Rica

*Heliconia Society International Plant Conservation Center

# Sources of Information on *Heliconia*

Readers interested in finding out more about the botany and horticulture of *Heliconia* should check the references given below. This list emphasizes the most recent publications and is not exhaustive, but it furnishes initial access to important literature sources.

## BOTANICAL PUBLICATIONS

Abalo, J. E., and L. G. Morales. 1982. Veintecinco (25) heliconias nuevas de Colombia. Phytologia 51: 1–61.
——— and ———. 1983. Doce (12) heliconias nuevas del Ecuador. Phytologia 52: 387–413.
Andersson, L. 1981 Revision of *Heliconia* sect. *Heliconia* (Musaceae). Nordic J. Bot. 1: 759–784.
———. 1985a. Revision of *Heliconia* subgen. *Stenochlamys* (Musaceae–Heliconioideae). Opera Bot. 82: 5–123.
———. 1985b. Musaceae. Fl. Ecuador 22: 3–87.
Aristeguieta, L. 1961. El genero *Heliconia* in Venezuela. Instituto Botanico, Caracas.
Barreiros, H. S. 1979. Heliconias com inflorescencia pendula (Heliconiaceae). Rodriguésia 31: 259–268.
Daniels, G. S., and F. G. Stiles. 1979. The *Heliconia* taxa of Costa Rica. Keys and descriptions. Brenesia 15(Supl.): 1–150.

Emygdio, L. de Mello Filho. 1975. O gênero *Heliconia* na flora fluminensis de Frei José Mariano da Conceiçao Vellozo. Revista Brasil Biol. 35: 331–337.

Kress, W. J. 1984. Systematics of Central American *Heliconia* (Heliconiaceae) with pendent inflorescences. J. Arnold Arbor. 65: 429–532.

———. 1985. Bat pollination of an Old World *Heliconia*. Biotropica 17: 302–308.

———. 1986. New heliconias (Heliconiaceae) from Panama. Selbyana 9: 156–166.

———. 1990. The taxonomy of Old World *Heliconia* (Heliconiaceae). Allertonia 6(1): 1–58.

Santos, E. 1978. Revisao das espécies do gênero *Heliconia* L. (Musaceae s.l.) espontâneas na regiao Fluminense. Rodriguésia 30: 99–221.

Smith, R. R. 1968. A taxonomic revision of the genus *Heliconia* in Middle America. Ph.D. dissertation. University of Florida, Gainesville. (Available from University Microfilms, Ann Arbor, MI.)

Stiles, F. G. 1979. Notes on the natural history of *Heliconia* (Musaceae) in Costa Rica. Brenesia 15(Supl.): 151–180.

———. 1980. Further data on the genus *Heliconia* (Musaceae) in northern Costa Rica. Brenesia 18: 147–154.

———. 1982. Taxonomic and distributional notes on Costa Rican *Heliconia* (Musaceae), II: Parque Nacional Braulio Carrillo, Cordillera Central. Brenesia 19/20: 221–230.

HORTICULTURAL PUBLICATIONS

Armbruster, J. 1974. *Heliconia psittacorum*—eine interessante Schnittblume aus der Familie de Bananengewachse. Gartnerbauliche Versuchbericht, pp. 175–178.

Ball, D. 1986. Hues of heliconia. Interior Landscape Industry 3(8): 25–29.

Broschat, T. K., and H. M. Donselman. 1983. Heliconias: a promising new cut flower crop. HortScience 18: 2.

——— and ———. 1983. Production and postharvest culture of *Heliconia psittacorum* flowers in South Florida. Proc. Fla. State Hort. Soc. 96: 272–273.

————, ————, and A. A. Will. 1984. Golden Torch, an orange heliconia for cut-flower use. Agriculture Experiment Stations, Univ. Florida IFAS, Circ. S-308.

————, ————, and ————. 1984. Andromeda, a red and orange heliconia for cut-flower use. Agriculture Experiment Stations, Univ. Florida IFAS, Circ. S-309.

Criley, R. A. 1985. Heliconias. Pp. 125–129. *In* Handbook of Flowering II. A. H. Halevy, ed. CRC Press, Inc., Boca Raton, FL, U.S.A.

———— and S. Lekawatana. 1987. Height control for potted *Heliconia stricta*. HortScience 23: 751.

Donselman, H. M., and T. K. Broschat. 1986. Heliconias for South Florida. Fairchild Trop. Gard. Bull. 41: 20–23.

———— and ————. 1987. Commercial heliconia production in South Florida. Nurserymen's Digest January: 49–52.

Fairchild Tropical Garden Bulletin. Volume 41, Number 1, January, 1986. (Issue with articles on "Heliconias—how to choose them, how to grow them, cut flowers.")

Heliconia Society International Bulletin, HSI Headquarters, c/o Flamingo Gardens, 3750 Flamingo Road, Ft. Lauderdale, FL 33330, U.S.A. (Quarterly bulletin with articles on botany, horticulture, and commercial aspects as well as Society news.)

Sterkel, R. 1987. Heliconia. Deutsch. Gartenb. 41: 2188–2190.

van Raalte, D., and D. van Raalte-Wichers. 1973. Heliconia. Vakblad Bloem. 28: 12–13.

Watson, D. P., and R. R. Smith. 1974. Ornamental heliconias. Univ. Hawaii Coop. Ext. Serv., Circ. 482.

Watson, J. B. 1986. Heliconias, a new challenge for landscape design. Fairchild Trop. Gard. Bull. 41: 6–19.

# Correct Names for Heliconias Listed in Other Horticultural Publications

The confusion over the correct names of heliconias is in part due to early misidentifications furnished in several standard horticultural books (*Tropica* [Second Edition], *Exotica* [Series 4], *Hortus Third*, and the *RHS Dictionary of Gardening* [Second Edition]). As an aid for those using these texts, a list of the names referring to photographs or descriptions supplied in these sources together with the correct botanical and horticultural names is given below. In some cases (indicated by a question mark in the lists), it is impossible to accurately identify the form or species described or listed.

Two color posters illustrating many cultivated heliconias have been commercially produced and distributed. The first, entitled "Exotic Tropical Flowers," was produced by Alii Gardens in Hana, Hawaii. Many new cultivar and common names were introduced in that poster. Readers are referred to an article by Kress and Baker (HSI Bulletin 3(2): 3, 1988) that lists the heliconias included in that poster and gives the correct names. The second poster was produced by Costa Flores of Costa Rica, Central America, and is entitled "The Farms of Costa Flores." Comments on the cultivar names used in that poster are provided in our section "Taxonomic Notes."

# HELICONIAS LISTED IN *TROPICA* (SECOND EDITION)

| *Tropica* Name (page number) | Correct Name |
|---|---|
| *acuminata* cv. Espiritu Santo (p. 664) | *angusta* Vell. cv. Orange Christmas |
| *aurantiaca* (p. 665) | *aurantiaca* Ghiesbr. ex. Lemaire |
| *bicolor* (p. 666) | *angusta* Vell. cv. Holiday |
| *bihai* cv. Firebird (p. 663) | *champneiana* Griggs cv. Maya Blood |
| *bourgaeana* (p. 667) | *bourgaeana* Peters. |
| *brasiliensis* cv. False bird-of-paradise (p. 665) | *angusta* Vell. cv. Holiday |
| *caribaea* cv. Lobster claw (p. 664) | *caribaea* Lam. cv. Purpurea |
| *caribaea* cv. Purpurea (p. 665) | *caribaea* Lam. cv. Purpurea |
| *caribaea* cv. Purpurea (p. 663) | *bihai* (L.) L. cv. Lobster Claw One |
| *caribaea* "Wild plantain" (p. 663) | *caribaea* Lam. cv. Gold |
| *collinsiana* (p. 666) | *collinsiana* Griggs var. *collinsiana* |
| *distans* (p. 663) | *latispatha* Benth. cv. Distans |
| *humilis* cv. Lobster claw (p. 663) | *bihai* (L.) L. cv. Lobster Claw One |
| *humilis* cv. Macaw flowers (p. 667) | *bihai* (L.) L. cv. Lobster Claw One |
| *illustris* cv. Aureo-striata (p. 668) | *indica* Lam. cv. Striata |
| *illustris* cv. Rubra (pp. 664, 668) | *indica* Lam. cv. Spectabilis |
| *illustris rubricaulis* (p. 668) | *indica* Lam. cv. Spectabilis |

| *Tropica* Name (page number) | Correct Name |
|---|---|
| *indica* (p. 668) | *indica* Lam. |
| | cv. Spectabilis |
| *jacquinii* (p. 663) | *caribaea* Lam. × bihai (L.) L. |
| | cv. Jacquinii |
| *latispatha* (pp. 663, 664) | *latispatha* Benth. |
| | cv. Orange Gyro |
| *marginata* (p. 665) | *rostrata* R.&P. |
| *mariae* (pp. 664, 666) | *mariae* J.D. Hook. |
| *platystachys* (p. 664) | *platystachys* Baker |
| *psittacorum* (p. 664) | *psittacorum* L.f. |
| | cv. Choconiana |
| *psittacorum* cv. Parrot flower (p. 666) | *psittacorum* L.f. × spathocircinata Aristeg. |
| | cv. Golden Torch |
| *psittacorum* cv. Parrot flowers (p. 664) | *psittacorum* L.f. |
| | cv. Choconiana |
| *psittacorum* cv. Rubra (p. 666) | *psittacorum* L.f. |
| | cv. Andromeda |
| *psittacorum rhizomatosa* cv. Parakeet flower (p. 666) | *psittacorum* L.f. |
| | cv. Sassy |
| *revoluta* (p. 663) | *nutans* Woodson |
| *rostrata* (pp. 666, 667) | *rostrata* R.&P. |
| *schiedeana* (p. 667) | *spissa* Griggs |
| *sharonii* (p. 668) | *stricta* Huber |
| | cv. Cooper's Sharonii |
| *spectabilis* (p. 664) | *indica* Lam. |
| | cv. Spectabilis |
| *spectabilis* cv. Edwardus Rex (p. 668) | *indica* Lam. |
| | cv. Spectabilis |
| *vellerigera* (p. 669) | *mutisiana* Cuatrecasas |
| *wagneriana* (pp. 663, 666, 673) | *wagneriana* Peters. |

## HELICONIAS LISTED IN *EXOTICA* (SERIES 4)

| *Exotica* Name (page number) | Correct Name |
|---|---|
| *acuminata* cv. Espiritu Santo (p. 1589) | *angusta* Vell. cv. Orange Christmas |
| *angustifolia* (*braziliensis*) (p. 1590) | *angusta* Vell. cv. Holiday |
| *aurantiaca* (pp. 1590, 1591, 1592) | *aurantiaca* Ghiesbr. ex Lemaire |
| *bihai* (p. 1588) | *bihai* (L.) L. cv. Lobster Claw One |
| *caribaea* (p. 1587) | *caribaea* Lam. cv. Purpurea |
| *caribaea* var. *purpurea* (p. 1588) | *caribaea* Lam. cv. Purpurea |
| *caribaea* (p. 1590) | *caribaea* Lam. cv. Gold |
| *caribaea* (p. 1592) | *latispatha* Benth. |
| *choconiana* (p. 1588) | *aurantiaca* Ghiesbr. ex Lemaire |
| *collinsiana* (p. 1592) | *collinsiana* Griggs var. *collinsiana* |
| *distans* (p. 1592) | *latispatha* Benth. cv. Distans |
| *elongata* (p. 1592) | *wagneriana* Peters. |
| *hirsuta* (p. 1590) | *hirsuta* L.f. |
| *humilis* (p. 1587) | *bihai* (L.) L. cv. Lobster Claw One |
| *humilis* (p. 1590) | *bihai* (L.) L. |
| *illustris* cv. Aureo-striata (pp. 1591, 1592) | *indica* Lam. cv. Striata |
| *illustris* cv. Edwardus Rex (p. 1591) | *indica* Lam. cv. Spectabilis |
| *illustris* cv. Rubra (p. 1592) | *indica* cv. Spectabilis |

| *Exotica* Name (page number) | Correct Name |
|---|---|
| *illustris* rubricaulis (pp. 1591, 1592) | *indica* Lam. cv. Spectabilis |
| *illustris* spectabilis (p. 1591) | *indica* Lam. cv. Spectabilis |
| *jacquinii* (p. 1590) | *bihai* (L.) L. cv. Lobster Claw One |
| *latispatha* (pp. 1588, 1590, 1591) | *latispatha* Benth. |
| *mariae* (p. 1592) | *mariae* J.D. Hook. |
| *metallica* (pp. 1590, 1591) | *metallica* Pl. & Lind. ex Hook. |
| *platystachys* (p. 1587) | *platystachys* Baker |
| *psittacorum* (p. 1588) | *psittacorum* L.f. cv. Sassy |
| *rostrata* cv. Hanging lobster-claws (p. 1589) | *rostrata* R. & P. |
| *velutina* (p. 1591) | ? (not *velutina* L. Anderss.) |

## HELICONIAS LISTED IN *HORTUS THIRD*

| *Hortus Third* Name | Correct Name |
|---|---|
| *amazonica* | ? |
| *angustifolia* | *angusta* Vell. |
| *aurantiaca* | *aurantiaca* Ghiesbr. ex Lemaire |
| *aureostriata* | *indica* Lam. cv. Striata |
| *bicolor* | *angusta* Vell. |
| *Bihai* | *bihai* (L.) L. |
| *brasiliensis* | *farinosa* Raddi |
| *caribaea* | *caribaea* Lam. |
| *coccinea* | ? |
| *Collinsiana* | *collinsiana* Griggs |
| *curtispatha* | *curtispatha* Peters. |

| Hortus Third Name | Correct Name |
|---|---|
| distans | ? |
| Edwardus-Rex | indica Lam. cv. Spectabilis |
| elongata | wagneriana Peters. |
| flava | ? |
| humilis | bihai (L.) L. (includes stricta Huber) |
| illustris | indica Lam. cv. Spectabilis |
| indica var. aureostriata | indica Lam. cv. Striata |
| Jacquinii | ? |
| latispatha | latispatha Benth. |
| Mariae | mariae J.D. Hook. |
| metallica | metallica Pl. & Lind. ex Hook. |
| osaensis | osaënsis Cuf. |
| pendula | collinsiana Griggs |
| platystachys | platystachys Baker and collinsiana Griggs |
| psittacorum | psittacorum L.f. |
| rostrata | rostrata R.&P. |
| rubra | ? |
| Schiedeana | schiedeana Kl. |
| Schneeana | meridensis Kl. |
| speciosa | farinosa Raddi |
| spectabilis | indica Lam. cv. Spectabilis |
| striata | indica Lam. cv. Striata |
| stricta | ? |
| velutina | ? |
| wagneriana | wagneriana Peters. |

## HELICONIAS LISTED IN THE *RHS DICTIONARY OF GARDENING* (SECOND EDITION)

| *RHS* Name | Correct Name |
| --- | --- |
| *angustifolia* | *angusta* Vell. |
| *aurantiaca* | *aurantiaca* Ghiesbr. ex Lemaire |
| *aureo-striata* | *indica* Lam. cv. Striata |
| *bicolor* | *angusta* Vell. |
| *Bihai* | *bihai* (L.) L. |
| *Bihai* var. *aureo-striata* | *indica* Lam. cv. Striata |
| *brasiliensis* | *farinosa* Raddi |
| *brevispatha* | *aurantiaca* Ghiesbr. ex Lemaire |
| *choconiana* | *aurantiaca* Ghiesbr. ex Lemaire |
| *elongata* | *wagneriana* Peters. |
| *farinosa* | *farinosa* Raddi |
| *humilis* | *bihai* (L.) L. |
| *illustris* | *indica* Lam. cv. Spectabilis |
| *illustris* var. *Edwardus Rex* | *indica* Lam. cv. Spectabilis |
| *illustris* var. *rubricaulis* | *indica* Lam. cv. Spectabilis |
| *indica* | *indica* Lam. |
| *marantifolia* | *metallica* Pl. & Lind. ex Hook. |
| *metallica* | *metallica* Pl. & Lind. ex Hook. |
| *psittacorum* | *psittacorum* L.f. |
| *Sanderi* | *indica* Lam. cv. Sanderi |
| *triumphans* | *Phrynium villosulum* Miq. (Marantaceae) |
| *vinosa* | *metallica* Pl. & Lind. ex Hook. |
| *wagneriana* | *wagneriana* Peters. |

# Taxonomic Notes

These notes on the origin and authorities of the names of species, hybrids, varieties, and cultivars of *Heliconia* are provided as additional explanations for the names selected here. Because of the past, current, and possible future proliferation and confusion of names, we have added this section to give some rationale and historical perspective to the names provided in this guide and to assist in identifying some names that have been used in the past.

Species names are listed alphabetically; cultivar and varietal names appear alphabetically within species. Hybrids are listed in alphabetical sequence under the first species name of the hybrid pair.

We have made a considerable effort to include in this book the legitimate botanical Latin names and the cultivar names that have the widest usage among horticulturists. In this section we use *follows* if the botanical or horticultural name has been published. Many of the articles cited have appeared in the *Bulletin* of the Heliconia Society International (HSI Bulletin); in these cases, the volume, issue, page, and year of the *Bulletin* are given in parentheses following the author(s). Other citations, in which only the author's name and year are given, can be found in the section "Sources of Information on *Heliconia*."

Many cultivar names cited here have not been published. In some cases we have been able to track down the person who first *applied* the name that is accepted here. In other instances cultivar names are cited that have been commonly *used*, but whose exact origins are unclear. In cases where a second cultivar name exists, we indicate that the plants have been secondarily *labeled* with this name in a particular region.

NOTES

*H. acuminata.* Some cultivars of this species have been incorrectly labeled in the past as belonging to *H. psittacorum*; hybrids between the two species undoubtedly exist (Andersson, 1985a).

*H. acuminata* cv. Cheri R. Cultivar name applied by J. Kress, February 1990.

*H. acuminata* cv. Ruby. Cultivar name follows D. Carli, 1988; earlier applied by B. Ramsaroop. Has been labeled Zodiac Red in Costa Rica.

*H. acuminata* cv. Taruma. Cultivar name applied by F. Berry and R. Baker, October 1988.

*H. acuminata* cv. Yellow Waltz. Cultivar name applied by F. Berry, October 1988.

*H. aemygdiana* ssp. *aemygdiana*. Follows Andersson (1985b). Labeled Salvador Dali Neon in Costa Rica.

*H. aemygdiana* ssp. *transandina*. Follows Andersson (1985b). Has been labeled Enchanted Forest in Costa Rica.

*H. angusta* cv. Holiday. Cultivar name applied by D. Ball and follows Kress and Baker (HSI Bulletin 3(2): 3, 1988). Imported to Florida by Bob Wilson as *H. brasiliensis*. Has been labeled Christmas, Red Xmas, and Red Christmas.

*H. angusta* cv. Orange Christmas. Cultivar name used in Hawaii; follows Kress and Baker (HSI Bulletin 3(2):3, 1988), except "aff." is deleted and Xmas is spelled out. Has also been labeled Pagoda, *H. citrina,* and *H.* aff. *flava.* Called Orange Holiday in Hawaii and tagged Espiritu Santo from Venezuela.

*H. angusta* cv. Yellow Christmas. Cultivar name used in Hawaii; follows Kress and Baker (HSI Bulletin 3(2): 3, 1988), except "aff." is deleted and Xmas is spelled out. Has been labeled *H. flava* or Flava; called Yellow Holiday in Hawaii. This form may correspond to the species *H. citrina* L. Emygdio & E. Santos.

*H. atropurpurea.* Follows Daniels and Stiles (1979). An interesting form of this species has been found in Costa Rica and is in cultivation in Florida under the name Stupendous. It lacks the maroon color on the lower surface of the leaf blade and blooms December through February.

*H. aurantiaca.* Follows Andersson (1985a) and Kress and Baker (HSI Bulletin 3(2): 3, 1988).

*H. beckneri* cv. Hall Red. Cultivar name applied by F. Berry, July 1989.

*H. beckneri* cv. Yellow Gyre. Cultivar name applied by F. Berry, July 1989.

*H. bella.* Follows Kress (1986).

*H. bihai.* At this time in the study of *Heliconia* taxonomy, we consider *H. bihai* to be a complex and diverse species composed of probably more than two dozen forms, 20 of which are included in this guide. In a number of prior taxonomic publications, several of the forms we treat here as cultivars were described as distinct species. Andersson (1981) correctly called *H. bihai* "a very polymorphic species," but did not have the advantage of seeing different clones from the wild reproducing themselves in cultivation. The taxonomic situation is made more complex by the apparent hybridization of this species with *H. caribaea* in the West Indies (Berry and Carli, HSI Bulletin 3(4): 4–5, 1988; Hirano, HSI Bulletin 4(1): 4–5, 1989).

*H. bihai* cv. Arawak. Cultivar name applied by F. Berry and J. Criswick, August 1987. The cultivar name Pont Casse has been used by T. Robinson in Dominica. A similar or the same form has been labeled 1950 Red in Costa Rica. The name Manoa Sunrise and its synonyms Red Bihai and Sunrise as used in Hawaii may be the same cultivar. A recent and intense survey in Grenada showed this form to be variable in the wild and in cultivation.

*H. bihai* cv. Aurea. Cultivar name follows Berry and Carli (HSI Bulletin 3(4): 4–5, 1988).

*H. bihai* cv. Balisier. Cultivar name comes from the common epithet used for this form in Trinidad; follows Berry and Carli (HSI Bulletin 3(4): 4–5, 1988). Has been labeled Claw 3 and Trinidad Balisier in Hawaii, Tobago in Costa Rica, and *H. bihai* ssp. *bihai* in Florida.

*H. bihai* cv. Banana Split. Cultivar name applied by D. Carli and follows Berry and Carli (HSI Bulletin 3(4): 4–5, 1988).

*H. bihai* cv. Chocolate Dancer. Cultivar name applied by J. Kress and follows Berry and Carli (HSI Bulletin 3(4): 4–5, 1988). A similar form has been labeled Dark Chocolate in Costa Rica.

*H. bihai* cv. Emerald Forest. Cultivar name applied by D. Carli and follows Berry and Carli (HSI Bulletin 3(4): 4–5, 1988).

*H. bihai* cv. Five A.M. Cultivar name applied by D. Carli, January 1988, and used incorrectly by Berry and Carli (HSI Bulletin 3(4): 4–5, 1988). Has been erroneously classed as a hybrid of *H. caribaea* × *H. bihai.*

*H. bihai* cv. Giant Lobster Claw. Cultivar name used in Hawaii and follows Kress and Baker (HSI Bulletin 3(2): 3, 1988). Previously labeled Tobago Yellow in Costa Rica and Claw 3, Yellow and Orange Claw, Trinidad Balisier, and Choconiana in Hawaii.

*H. bihai* cv. Hatchet. Cultivar name applied by F. Berry in 1987 and follows Berry and Carli (HSI Bulletin 3(4): 4–5, 1988).

*H. bihai* cv. Jaded Forest. Cultivar name applied by D. Carli and follows Berry and Carli (HSI Bulletin 3(4): 4–5, 1988). The cultivar names Green Dancer, Green Bihai, and St. Lucia Green have been used.

*H. bihai* cv. Kamehameha. Cultivar name used in Hawaii and applied by Kress and Baker (HSI Bulletin 3(2): 3, 1988). Has been called Stripe.

*H. bihai* cv. Kuma Negro. Cultivar name applied by D. Carli, June 1988. A lighter form has been labeled Kuma in Costa Rica.

*H. bihai* cv. Lobster Claw One. Cultivar name used in Hawaii, *fide* R. Baker, October 1988. Has been labeled Schneana in Costa Rica. Two growth forms exist in cultivation in Costa Rica, each probably representing distinct cultivars called Schneana Grand Papa and Schneana Grand Mama.

*H. bihai* cv. Lobster Claw Two. Cultivar name used in Hawaii and given as Claw 2 by Kress and Baker (HSI Bulletin 3(2): 3, 1988). Also known as Schneana or Scheana and as Red-stemmed Lobster and Year-round Lobster in Hawaii.

*H. bihai* cv. Nappi. Cultivar name applied by D. Carli and follows Berry and Carli (HSI Bulletin 3(2): 3, 1988).

*H. bihai* cv. Nappi Yellow. Cultivar name applied by D. Carli and follows Berry (HSI Bulletin 4(2): 11, 1989). This form has been recognized as a distinct species, *H. adeliana* L. Emygdio & E. Santos.

*H. bihai* cv. Purple Throat. Cultivar name applied by D. Carli and follows Berry and Carli (HSI Bulletin 3(4): 4–5, 1988).

*H. bihai* cv. Schaefer's Bihai. This form was described as a distinct species from Venezuela, *H. schaeferiana* Rodriguez, but is now placed in synonymy with *H. bihai* by Aristeguieta (1961) and Andersson (1981). The cultivar name is used here for the first time.

*H. bihai* cv. Swish. This cultivar has been transferred to *H. stricta*.

*H. bihai* cv. Yellow Dancer. Cultivar name applied by J. Kress in 1987 and follows Berry and Carli (HSI Bulletin 3(4): 4–5, 1988). Has been called Yellow Bihai and St. Vincent Yellow in Hawaii; labeled Island Yellow in Costa Rica.

*H. bihai* × *H. spathocircinata* cv. Cinnamon Twist. Cultivar name and hybrid combination applied by D. Carli in 1988.

*H. bourgaeana*. Follows Kress and Baker (HSI Bulletin 3(2): 3, 1988). In Hawaii has been labeled Purple Bourgaeana, Purple Heliconia, Rosea Bourgaeana, and Rose. Also called Virjon. Has been labeled Panty Pink in Costa Rica.

*H. calatheaphylla*. Follows Daniels and Stiles (1979) and Andersson (1985a).

*H. caribaea*. A number of distinct forms and cultivars of this species have been recognized for some time, especially by growers and specialists in Hawaii, Costa Rica, and Florida. We list seven of the more impressive cultivars in this guide, and are aware of several other forms that need more study. See Berry and Carli (HSI Bulletin 3(4): 4–5, 1988). This species hybridizes with *H. bihai.*

*H. caribaea* cv. Barbados Flat. Cultivar name applied by D. Carli, May 1989.

*H. caribaea* cv. Black Magic. Cultivar name applied by D. Carli and follows Berry and Carli (HSI Bulletin 3(4): 4–5, 1988).

*H. caribaea* cv. Chartreuse. Cultivar name used in Hawaii *fide* R. Baker, October 1988. Labeled Lemon Drop; a similar form named Persian Eyes in Costa Rica.

*H. caribaea* cv. Cream. Cultivar name used in Hawaii and follows Kress and Baker (HSI Bulletin 3(2): 3, 1988). Has been labeled Light Cream in Costa Rica.

*H. caribaea* cv. Flash. Cultivar name used in Hawaii *fide* R. Baker, October 1988, and listed by Berry and Carli (HSI Bulletin 3(4): 4–5, 1988).

*H. caribaea* cv. Gold. Cultivar name used in Hawaii *fide* R. Baker, October 1988. Has been called Wild Plantain in Martinique and Wild Plantation, Caribaea, and Yellow Caribaea in Hawaii. Slightly different color phases, possibly distinct cultivars, have been called Summer Gold and St. Vincent Yellow. Has been labeled Jamaican Yellow in Costa Rica.

*H. caribaea* cv. Purpurea. Cultivar name used for some time, especially in Hawaii; follows Kress and Baker (HSI Bulletin 3(2): 3, 1988). Has also been less commonly called Burgundy, Red Caribaea, and Red Caribe in Hawaii and possibly Volcano Red in Costa Rica. Several color variants are currently lumped under Purpurea but may eventually be recognized as distinct cultivars.

*H. caribaea* × *H. bihai.* This set of (presumed) hybrids was discussed by Berry and Carli (HSI Bulletin 3(4): 4–5, 1988) and supporting data were given by Hirano (HSI Bulletin 4(1): 4–5, 1989). We describe ten cultivated hybrids, and are aware that others exist.

*H. caribaea* × *H. bihai* cv. Carib Flame. Cultivar name applied by J. Criswick and follows Criswick (HSI Bulletin 4(1): 1–2, 1989).

*H. caribaea* × *H. bihai* cv. Criswick. Cultivar name applied by F. Berry; follows Berry and Carli (HSI Bulletin 3(4): 4–5, 1988) and

Criswick (HSI Bulletin 4(1): 1–2, 1989). This form has previously been referred to as Blaize in Grenada.

*H. caribaea* × *H. bihai* cv. Grand Etang. Cultivar name applied by F. Berry and A. Carle, August 1989.

*H. caribaea* × *H. bihai* cv. Green Thumb. Cultivar name applied by D. Carli, July 1988.

*H. caribaea* × *H. bihai* cv. Grenadier. Cultivar name applied by J. Criswick and follows Criswick (HSI Bulletin 4(1): 1–2, 1989).

*H. caribaea* × *H. bihai* cv. Jacquinii. This form has been considered a distinct species by some, or a synonym or cultivar of *H. bihai* by others. It was treated as a cultivar of this hybrid by Kress and Baker (HSI Bulletin 3(2): 3, 1988) and Criswick (HSI Bulletin 4(1): 1–2, 1989). Also known as Giant Jamaican, Rainbow, O'Sullivan, Red & Yellow Lobster, and sometimes Aurea in Hawaii.

*H. caribaea* × *H. bihai* cv. Kawauchi. Cultivar name used in Hawaii *fide* R. Baker, October 1988, reportedly as a seedling from a red *H. caribaea.*

*H. caribaea* × *H. bihai* cv. Richmond Red. Cultivar name probably applied by Iris Bannochie after Richmond Valley, St. Vincent. Used since 1980 in Hawaii, and documented as a probable hybrid by Hirano (HSI Bulletin 4(1): 4–5, 1989). Formerly called Red Bihai in Hawaii, and may be the form called Purpurea II. A similar (or the same) cultivar is labeled St. Marks Red on Grenada.

*H. caribaea* × *H. bihai* cv. Vermillion Lake. Cultivar name applied by John Criswick prior to July 1987 and follows Criswick (HSI Bulletin 4(1): 1–2, 1989).

*H. caribaea* × *H. bihai* cv. Yellow Dolly. Cultivar name applied by J. Criswick, August 1989. Previously labeled La Grenade or (in error) La Grenada.

*H. champneiana* cv. Maya Blood. Cultivar name applied by H. Bullis in 1987 and used since then in Florida. Has been labeled Firebird in Mexico.

*H. champneiana* cv. Maya Gold. Cultivar name applied by H. Bullis in 1987 and used since then in Florida. The cv. name of Honduras cited by Kress and Baker (HSI Bulletin 3(2): 3, 1988) for Hawaii, where it has also been called Cooper's Seed and Yellow Bourgaeana. Also called Mayan Gold.

*H. champneiana* cv. Splash. Cultivar name used for some time in Hawaii and Florida; follows Kress and Baker (HSI Bulletin 3(2): 3, 1988). Also had been called Freckles and Lucita Wait in Hawaii.

*H. chartacea* cv. Sexy Pink. Cultivar name said to have originated in Hawaii and now widely adopted. Also has been called *H. reticulata,* Roseo-pendula, and Flamingo.

*H. chartacea* cv. Sexy Scarlet. Cultivar name applied by Cristina Lindley in 1987; follows Kress and Baker (HSI Bulletin 3(2): 3, 1988). Has been called Maroon Chartacea and Sexy Burgundy in Hawaii and Marisa in Guyana.

*H. clinophila.* Follows Daniels and Stiles (1979).

*H. colgantea.* Follows Kress (1984). Has been labeled Flamingo in Costa Rica.

*H. collinsiana.* Follows Kress (1984) and Kress and Baker (HSI Bulletin 3(2): 3, 1988). Known as Red Hanging Heliconia and Pendula in Hawaii.

*H. curtispatha.* Follows Andersson (1985b).

*H. danielsiana.* Follows Kress (1984). Has been labeled King Kong in Costa Rica. Erroneously identified as *H. vellerigera* in Costa Rica by Daniels and Stiles (1979).

*H. densiflora* cv. Fire Flash. Cultivar name used in Hawaii *fide* R. Baker, October 1988, for a cultivar brought from Australia. Formerly thought to be a form of *H. psittacorum.*

*H. dielsiana.* Follows Andersson (1985b) and Kress (unpublished).

*H. episcopalis.* Follows Andersson (1985b). Different color phases have been reported, but have not yet been classified. Also called Spear, Arrow, and Gold Fish in Hawaii, and Prayer in Costa Rica.

*H.* × *flabellata* (*H. episcopalis* × *H. standleyi*). This form was described as a separate species by Abalo and Morales (1983). Its hybrid status and possible parents were first suggested by Andersson (1985b) and later applied by D. Carli, November 1988. The hybrid designation is accepted and applied here. Has been labeled Arrowhead in Costa Rica.

*H. gracilis.* At least four color forms have been found in Costa Rica; two of these are cultivated and described in this guide. Andersson (1985a) includes this species in *H. ignescens.*

*H. gracilis* cv. Gil Daniels. Cultivar name proposed here. Gilbert S. Daniels is past president of HSI and the senior author of the original species description of the red form.

*H. gracilis* cv. John Hall. Cultivar name applied by F. Berry, January 1988. John Hall brought the yellow form to our attention and cultivated it in Palmares, Costa Rica. Has been labeled Gracilis Yellow in Costa Rica.

*H. griggsiana* cv. Angry Moon. Cultivar name applied by D. Carli, January 1989. This form was recognized as a distinct species, *H. tandayapensis* Abalo and Morales.

*H. griggsiana* cv. Blue Moon. Cultivar name applied by D. Carli, January 1989. This form was recognized as a distinct species, *H. boultoniana* Abalo and Morales.

*H. hirsuta.* Andersson (1985a) regarded *H. hirsuta* as "a highly polymorphic" species with many color forms found throughout its geographic range. Nine of these forms now in cultivation are described in this guide. We have seen other cultivars. In some cases, cultivars of *H. hirsuta* have been labeled as *H. psittacorum.* Some have been described as distinct species (e.g., *H. burle-marxii* L. Emygdio).

*H. hirsuta* cv. Alicia. Cultivar name applied by F. Berry, February 1989.

*H. hirsuta* cv. Costa Flores. Cultivar name applied by F. Berry, November 1988. Labeled Subulata in Costa Rica.

*H. hirsuta* cv. Darrell. Cultivar name applied by F. Berry, October 1988.

*H. hirsuta* cv. Halloween. Cultivar name applied by F. Berry, October 1988.

*H. hirsuta* cv. Pancoastal. Cultivar name applied by F. Berry, February 1989. Had been labeled Burle-Marx in Florida.

*H. hirsuta* cv. Roberto Burle-Marx. Cultivar name applied by F. Berry, February 1989, as a cultivar in this species. Had been listed as a distinct species *H. burle-marxii,* a form of *H. psittacorum,* or as cv. Burle-Marx.

*H. hirsuta* cv. Trinidad Red. Cultivar name applied by F. Berry, May 1989. Labeled Trinidad in Costa Rica.

*H. hirsuta* cv. Twiggy. Cultivar name applied by F. Berry, February 1989.

*H. hirsuta* cv. Yellow Panama. Cultivar name applied by F. Berry, February 1989. Has been listed as *H. hirsuta* var. *hirsuta,* Yellow Psittacorum in Hawaii, and Panama Yellow in Costa Rica.

*H. ignescens.* Follows Daniels and Stiles (1979).

*H. imbricata.* Follows Daniels and Stiles (1979). Musubi has been used as a cultivar name in Hawaii. Several cultivars are known.

*H. imbricata* × *H. latispatha* cv. José Abalo. Cultivar name applied by F. Berry, May 1989. Labeled Stairway To Heaven in Costa Rica.

*H. imbricata* × *H. sarapiquensis* cv. Harvey Bullis. Cultivar name applied by F. Berry, May 1989. Named Bertha by J. Hall or Burtha by D. Carli.

*H. indica* var. *micholitzii.* Follows Kress and Baker (HSI Bulletin 3(2): 3, 1988) and Kress (1990).

*H. indica* var. *rubricarpa.* Follows Kress (1990).

*H. indica* cv. Rabaul. Follows Kress (1990). Has been called Domesticans.

*H. indica* cv. Spectabilis. Follows Kress (1990). Previously listed under a variety of cultivar and species names, including Spectabilis, Edwardus Rex, Illustris, Rubra, Pink-striped Heliconia, Rubricarpa, and Rubricaulis.

*H. indica* cv. Striata. Follows Kress (1990). Previously listed under other names, notably Aureo-striata. Has been called Yellow-striped Heliconia in Hawaii.

*H. irrasa* ssp. *irrasa*. Follows Daniels and Stiles (1979). Several color forms are known.

*H. irrasa* ssp. *undulata*. Follows Daniels and Stiles (1979).

*H. lanata*. Follows Kress (1990).

*H. lankesteri* var. *lankesteri*. Follows Daniels and Stiles (1979).

*H. lankesteri* var. *rubra*. Follows Daniels and Stiles (1979).

*H. lasiorachis*. Follows Andersson (1985a).

*H. latispatha*. There are many distinctive color phases of this species throughout its native geographic range. Three cultivars are described here.

*H. latispatha* cv. Distans. Although Distans was originally published as a synonym of *H. bihai*, it has been consistently applied to a cultivar of *H. latispatha*. To preserve its wide use as a cultivar name, it is accepted here for a small form (less than 4 ft. tall) of *H. latispatha*. Follows Kress and Baker (HSI Bulletin 3(2): 3, 1988).

*H. latispatha* cv. Red-yellow Gyro. Cultivar name applied and used here. This is similar to Latispatha Pastel Pink labeled from Costa Rica.

*H. latispatha* cv. Orange Gyro. Cultivar name applied and used here. Has been labeled Yellow & Gold in Costa Rica.

*H. laufao*. Follows Kress (1990).

*H. lennartiana*. Follows Kress (1986). Has been labeled Lenny Pastel Yellow in Costa Rica.

*H. librata*. Follows Kress (unpublished). Labeled Desert Sands in Costa Rica.

*H. lindsayana*. Follows Kress (1986). Three color forms are known to exist in cultivation.

*H. lingulata* cv. Fan. Cultivar name follows Kress and Baker (HSI Bulletin 3(2): 3, 1988). Fan has been restricted in Hawaii to the yellow-chartreuse form (also called Candelabra or Yellow Fan). Red-Tip Fan has been used in Hawaii for the form with salmon-orange bracts. Labeled Southern Cross in Costa Rica and possibly as Yellow Lance.

*H. lingulata* cv. Spiral Fan. Cultivar name applied and used here for spiral form of the distichous *H. lingulata;* not the same as *H. pseudoaemygdiana* cv. Birdiana.

*H. longa.* Follows Daniels and Stiles (1979) and Andersson (1985b).

*H. longiflora.* Follows Daniels and Stiles (1979). Two color forms are known.

*H. lophocarpa.* Follows Daniels and Stiles (1979).

*H. lutea.* Follows Kress (1986).

*H. magnifica.* Follows Kress (1984).

*H. marginata.* Follows Kress (1984). The common form (bracts red with yellow lip) is described here. A yellow-bracted form also exists (Aristeguieta, 1961).

*H. mariae.* Follows Kress (1984). Called Beefsteak Heliconia in Hawaii and Firecracker in Costa Rica.

*H. mariae* × *H. pogonantha* var. *holerythra* cv. Bushmaster. Cultivar name applied and used here.

*H. mathiasiae.* Taxonomic confusion exists in the Central American complex of *H. mathiasiae–deflexa–vaginalis–golfodulcensis–wilsonii* (Andersson, 1985a). *Heliconia mathiasiae* includes several forms (two described in this guide) found from Mexico to Costa Rica, while *H. vaginalis* (including *H. deflexa* and probably *H. golfodulcensis*) is found in Costa Rica south to Colombia.

*H. mathiasiae* cv. Mildred. Cultivar name for a Costa Rican form adopted and used here.

*H. mathiasiae* cv. Pacal. Cultivar name for a form from Mexico to Nicaragua adopted and used here.

*H. metallica.* Follows Andersson (1985a). At least two forms occur *fide* G. Stiles (pers. comm.). The typical *metallica* form is described here.

*H. monteverdensis.* Follows Daniels and Stiles (1979) and Stiles (1980). Two varieties: var. *monteverdensis* described here with red bracts and var. *volcanicola* with yellow bracts (HSI Bulletin 4(4): 9, 1990).

*H. mutisiana.* Follows Kress and Baker (HSI Bulletin 3(2): 3, 1988). Has been called Fuzzy Pink Hanging in Hawaii and labeled Pink Panther in Costa Rica.

*H. necrobracteata.* Follows Kress (1984).

*H. × nickeriensis (H. psittacorum × H. marginata).* This hybrid was originally described as a species, *H. nickeriensis,* from Suriname and is still so labeled at times. Has been called Nicky in Hawaii and Costa Rica and Nicky Spike in Costa Rica.

*H. nigripraefixa.* Follows Andersson (1985b).

*H. nutans.* Follows Kress (1984).

*H. orthotricha.* Follows Andersson (1985b). Sometimes incorrectly spelled "ortotricha." Two cultivars are described here.

*H. orthotricha* cv. Edge Of Nite. Cultivar name applied by D. Carli, July 1988. Tivaro Red has been used in Australia.

*H. orthotricha* cv. She. Cultivar name applied by D. Carli, 1988.

*H. osaënsis.* Follows Stiles (1980) as var. *osaensis;* Stiles also described var. *rubescens,* which was included in *H. metallica* by Andersson (1985a).

*H. paka.* Follows Kress (1990).

*H. papuana.* Follows Kress (1990).

*H. pastazae.* Follows Andersson (1985b). Previously called Ecuador in Hawaii.

*H. pendula* cv. Bright Red. Cultivar name applied by F. Berry, October 1988. Has been labeled Pendula Red in Costa Rica. This species is similar to and has been confused with *H. revoluta* from Venezuela. *Heliconia revoluta* has been applied to forms of *H. pendula* in Hawaii.

*H. pendula* cv. Frosty. Cultivar name originated in Hawaii *fide* R. Baker, October 1988, who reported that its seeds have germinated to produce all three cultivars described in this guide. This form has been recognized as a distinct species, *H. mariae-augustae* L. Emygdio and E. Santos.

*H. pendula* cv. Red Waxy. Cultivar name applied by F. Berry, October 1988. Has been labeled Orange Pelican in Costa Rica.

*H. platystachys.* Follows Kress (1984) and Kress and Baker (HSI Bulletin 3(2): 3, 1988). Has been called Red & Yellow Pendula in Hawaii and Sexy Orange in Hawaii and Costa Rica.

*H. pogonantha* var. *holerythra.* Follows Kress (1984).

*H. pogonantha* var. *pogonantha.* Follows Kress (1984). Labeled Pogo in Panama.

*H. pseudoaemygdiana* cv. Birdiana. Species name follows José Abalo (pers. comm., April 1989), although the botanical status of this form is not yet clear. It may be a hybrid of *H. lingulata* × *H. latispatha* or a variety of the former species. Previously labeled *H. lingulata* or *H. birdiana.* Cultivar name attributed to Howard Cooper pre-1980; also spelled Birdeyana. Labeled cv. Pagoda by Kress and Baker (HSI Bulletin 3(2): 3, 1988).

*H. psittacorum.* This diverse species from northern South America is made up of a large and impressive number of forms, many of which are cultivated. Estimates of numbers of natural forms range from 85 to 1,000(!). Only 14 cultivars, including the most commonly grown ones, are described here. A concerted descriptive study is warranted to document this diversity and to sort out the plethora of names applied to these cultivars.

*H. psittacorum* cv. Andromeda. Cultivar name applied by A. Will and H. Donselman in 1977, based on plants obtained from Andromeda Gardens, Barbados. A similar form with redder bracts and smaller inflorescences is grown in Denmark under the name Tay (Geersten, HSI Bulletin 4(1): 3, 1989).

*H. psittacorum* cv. Black Cherry. Cultivar name applied by H. Manley, October 1988.

*H. psittacorum* cv. Choconiana. Cultivar name used by D. Ball about 1984. Also known as Orange Psittacorum and Iao Beauty Dwarf in Hawaii. Small and large growth forms are alleged.

*H. psittacorum* cv. Fuchsia. Cultivar name used in Hawaii *fide* H. Manley, October 1988.

*H. psittacorum* cv. Kathy. Cultivar name used in Hawaii *fide* H. Manley, October 1988.

*H. psittacorum* cv. Lady Di. Cultivar name applied by C. Ullman and R. Wyss in 1985 to plants from Jamaica. Has been labeled Matchstick in Florida.

*H. psittacorum* cv. Lillian. Cultivar name used in Hawaii *fide* H. Manley, October 1988.

*H. psittacorum* cv. Parakeet. Cultivar name follows Kress and Baker (HSI Bulletin 3(2): 3, 1988). Called Rhizomatosa at times in Florida and Hawaii, also Dwarf Bird, Razzamatazz, and Parakeet Flower.

*H. psittacorum* cv. Peter Bacon. Cultivar name applied by F. Berry, April 1987.

*H. psittacorum* cv. St. Vincent Red. Cultivar name applied by Iris Bannonchie about 1972 on plants brought to Barbados from St. Vincent.

*H. psittacorum* cv. Sassy. Cultivar name applied by Lilian Oliveira and Ray Baker about 1983; follows Kress and Baker (HSI Bulletin 3(2): 3, 1988). Known as Kaleidoscope in Florida *fide* H. Donselman and T. Broschat, 1985.

*H. psittacorum* cv. Shamrock. Cultivar name applied by F. Berry, February 1989.

*H. psittacorum* cv. Strawberries and Cream. Name applied by H. Manley, October 1988. Has been labeled Strawberry & Cream in Costa Rica.

*H. psittacorum* cv. Suriname Sassy. Name applied by D. Carli, January 1988.

*H. psittacorum* × *H. spathocircinata* cv. Alan Carle. Cultivar name applied by F. Berry, January 1989. Labeled Golden Opal in Costa Rica. Slightly different forms cultivated in Dominican Republic and Venezuela.

*H. psittacorum* × *H. spathocircinata* cv. Golden Torch. Cultivar name applied by A. Will and H. Donselman in 1977 on the basis of plants brought to Florida from Andromeda Gardens, Barbados;

follows Kress and Baker (HSI Bulletin 3(2): 3, 1988). Called Parrot or Parrot flower in Hawaii and Yellow Bird in Florida and Jamaica.

*H. psittacorum* × *H. spathocircinata* cv. Golden Torch Adrian. Cultivar name applied by D. Carli, January 1989. Has been labeled Red Golden Torch in Costa Rica.

*H. ramonensis*. Follows Kress (1984); four varieties have been described. A form of this from Panama is called Rambo in Costa Rica.

*H.* × *rauliniana* (*H. marginata* × *H. bihai*). Follows use in Brazil and Venezuela *fide* José Abalo, April 1989, except that we consider it a hybrid and so apply that designation here.

*H. reticulata*. Follows Daniels and Stiles (1979).

*H. richardiana*. Follows Andersson (1985a). This species has also been called *H. glauca* Poiteau ex Verlot.

*H. rodriguensis*. Follows Aristeguieta (1961). There may be a morphological cline of gradation of this form into *H. bihai* cv. Lobster Claw One.

*H. rodriguezii*. Follows Stiles (1982).

*H. rostrata*. Follows Andersson (1985b) and Kress and Baker (HSI Bulletin 3(2): 3, 1988). Long in cultivation, this species has many different growth forms. A more careful examination of this variation is needed. Has been called Parrot's Beak and Twirl in Hawaii and forms have been labeled Five Day and Ten Day in Costa Rica. In Florida, the cultivar name Lobster Claw most commonly refers to this species.

*H. sarapiquensis*. Follows Daniels and Stiles (1979).

*H. schiedeana*. Follows Andersson (1985). Labeled Twist And Shout in Costa Rica.

*H. secunda*. There are two varieties of this species (Daniels and Stiles, 1979). Variety *secunda* from Costa Rica is described in this guide; the other form, also from Costa Rica, is var. *viridiflora* with green sepals.

*H. secunda* × *H. clinophila* cv. Toucan. Cultivar name applied by

F. Berry, May 1989. Hybrid status proposed by D. Carli, January 1989. Labeled Which Way Dego in Costa Rica.

*H. solomonensis.* Follows Kress (1990). Has been labeled Flag of the Empire in Costa Rica.

*H. spathocircinata.* Follows Aristeguieta (1961) and Andersson (1985b).

*H. spissa* cv. Guatemala Yellow. Cultivar name applied and used here.

*H. spissa* cv. Mexico Red. Cultivar name applied and used here.

*H. standleyi.* Follows Andersson (1985b). Has been labeled Rostrata Stanley in Costa Rica.

*H. stilesii.* Follows Kress (1984).

*H. stricta.* This species is polymorphic throughout its range in tropical South America. Of the 20 forms known to us, 16 in cultivation are described in this guide. In the past some forms of *H. stricta* have erroneously been called *H. humilis.*

*H. stricta* cv. Bob Wilson. Cultivar name applied by D. Carli, January 1989. Previously labeled Beta in Florida and Bob's Red in Costa Rica.

*H. stricta* cv. Bucky. Cultivar name applied by B. Ramsaroop, 1986. Also known as Guyana Red in Florida.

*H. stricta* cv. Carli's Sharonii. Cultivar name applied and used here.

*H. stricta* cv. Castanza. Cultivar name applied by F. Berry, October 1988.

*H. stricta* cv. Cochabamba. Cultivar name applied by F. Berry, October 1988.

*H. stricta* cv. Cooper's Sharonii. Cultivar name applied and used here. Called *H. stricta* cv. Sharonii by Kress and Baker (HSI Bulletin 3(2): 3, 1988). The various Sharonii cultivars are characterized by leaves with a maroon midrib on the upper surface and the lower surface all maroon. The earliest form we have tracked was brought to Helani Gardens, Maui, Hawaii, by H. Cooper from a grower named Sharon in Florida, about 1972; it still grows there.

*H. stricta* cv. Dimples. Cultivar name used in Hawaii *fide* Lilian Oliveira, June 1990, where it has also been labeled Orange and Yellow Stricta. Has been called Dwarf Tagami in Australia and Charlotte Yemane in Florida.

*H. stricta* cv. Dorado Gold. Cultivar name used by D. Carli, August 1989. Previously called Quito Gold in Costa Rica.

*H. stricta* cv. Dwarf Jamaican. Cultivar name used in Hawaii and elsewhere; follows Kress and Baker (HSI Bulletin 3(2): 3, 1988). This form has been called Dwarf Stricta, Dwarf Humilis, Mini-Jamaica, Jamaican, Dwarf Lobster, Humilis, Jamaican Red, and Dwarf Jamaican Light Red.

*H. stricta* cv. Dwarf Wag. Cultivar name applied here. Previously labeled Dwarf Wagneriana in Costa Rica.

*H. stricta* cv. Fire Bird. Cultivar name used in Hawaii and follows Kress and Baker (HSI Bulletin 3(2): 3, 1988). Previously labeled *H. brasiliensis,* Red Runs and Red Royal in Hawaii.

*H. stricta* cv. Las Cruces. Cultivar name applied by F. Berry, January 1988. Previously called Alpha in Florida.

*H. stricta* cv. Lee Moore. Cultivar name applied by F. Berry, January 1988.

*H. stricta* cv. Oliveira's Sharonii. Cultivar name applied and used here.

*H. stricta* cv. Petite. Cultivar name applied by D. Carli and F. Berry, January 1989. This cultivar was previously listed under *H. bihai.* Cultivar name applied by F. Berry, October 1988.

*H. stricta* cv. Tagami. Cultivar name long used in Hawaii. Listed as Royal by Kress and Baker (HSI Bulletin 3(2): 3, 1988). Also called Red & Yellow Runs in Hawaii.

*H. subulata.* Follows Andersson (1985a), who described two sub-species. A dark scarlet form is called Africa in Hawaii.

*H. talamancana.* Follows Kress (1984).

*H. thomasiana.* Follows Kress (1986). Two slightly different color phases have been cultivated. Has been labeled Mai Mai in Costa Rica.

*H. tortuosa* cv. Red Twist. Cultivar name applied by F. Berry, June 1989. A form of this is called Short Red in Hawaii. Has been called Tortuosa Red and Tortuosa Red & Yellow in Costa Rica, where two morphological forms of this color type may exist.

*H. tortuosa* cv. Yellow Twist. Cultivar name applied and used here.

*H. trichocarpa*. Follows Kress (1984). Has been labeled Red Cross in Costa Rica. Two varieties have been described in Costa Rica.

*H. umbrophila*. Follows Daniels and Stiles (1979).

*H. vaginalis*. This form of *H. vaginalis*, as restricted here by us, was described as a distinct species, *H. deflexa* Daniels and Stiles (see comment under *H. mathiasiae*). Other species or cultivars have been lumped into it by Andersson (1985a).

*H. vellerigera*. Follows Andersson (1985b). Has been labeled She Kong in Costa Rica.

*H. velloziana*. Has been called Arvum in Hawaii. The taxonomic boundaries between this species, *H. farinosa*, and *H. sampaioana*, all native to the Atlantic coastal rain forests of Brazil, are unclear at present.

*H. wagneriana*. Follows Daniels and Stiles (1979), Andersson (1981), and Kress and Baker (HSI Bulletin 3(2): 3, 1988). In Hawaii has been called Rainbow, Avenue, Elongata, Easter, and Easter Egg Flower. Somewhat different color forms have been named Torbo in Hawaii and Wagneriana Costa Flores in Costa Rica.

*H. wilsonii*. Follows Daniels and Stiles (1979). See comment under *H. mathiasiae*.

*H. xanthovillosa*. Follows Kress (1984). Several color phases exist; one has been labeled Shogun Golden Triangle and another Shogun Jade in Costa Rica.

*H. zebrina* cv. Inca. Cultivar name applied and used here.

*H. zebrina* cv. Tim Plowman. Although put here in *Heliconia zebrina*, this cultivar may be a form of *H. fugax* L. Anderss. Cultivar name applied by F. Berry and D. Sucre, February 1989.

# Glossary

[Many of the definitions provided below were adapted from the following sources: Lawrence, G. H. M., 1951, Taxonomy of Vascular Plants, The Macmillan Co., New York; and Lincoln, R. J., G. A. Boxshall, and P. F. Clark, 1982, A Dictionary of Ecology, Evolution and Systematics, Cambridge University Press.]

AMERICAN TROPICS.   A biogeographic region comprising South America, the West Indies, and Central America south of the Mexican Plateau; neotropics.

BINOMIAL.   The two-word scientific designation of a species, consisting of a generic name and a specific epithet.

BIOLOGICAL SPECIES.   Groups of actually or potentially interbreeding natural populations genetically isolated from other such groups by one or more reproductive isolating mechanisms.

BRACT.   A much reduced leaflike structure, usually associated with and subtending flowers. See also Inflorescence bract and Floral bract.

BRANCH BRACT.   See Inflorescence bract.

CANNOID.   A plant habit of certain heliconias in which the leaves have short- to medium-length petioles and obliquely held blades, resembling the shoot organization of cannas.

CHEEK.    The broad face of an inflorescence bract.

CINCINNAL BRACT.    See Inflorescence bract.

CLASSIFICATION.    A process of establishing, defining, and ranking taxa within hierarchical groups; a hierarchical series of taxa.

CLOUD FOREST.    A humid tropical forest at moderate to high elevations in which precipitation is in the form of clouds as well as rain.

CROSS-FERTILIZATION.    Fertilization resulting from the transfer of pollen from one flower to the stigma of a flower on another plant of the same species.

CULTIVAR.    Cultivated variety; an assemblage of cultivated plants which is clearly distinguished by certain characters and which, when reproduced, retains its distinguishing characters; abbreviated cv.

DISTAL.    Toward the apex.

DISTICHOUS.    Two ranked, with leaves or bracts on opposite sides of a stem or axis.

DRUPE.    A fleshy, few-seeded fruit with the seed enclosed in the stony inner layer of the fruit wall, like a peach.

ECOLOGY.    The study of the interrelationships between living organisms and their environment.

EMASCULATION.    The removal of the fertile, pollen-containing organs (anthers) of a flower to prevent self-pollination.

ENDEMIC.    Native to, and restricted to, a particular geographic region.

FAMILY.    A taxonomic category comprising one or more genera of common phylogenetic origin; the hierarchical rank that occurs between the genus and order.

FERTILIZATION.    The union of the male and female gametes to form a zygote; sometimes used more generally for the act of pollination.

FLORAL BRACT.    A modified leaflike structure subtending an individual flower within the inflorescence bracts of *Heliconia* and other members of the Zingiberales.

FLOWER.    The reproductive structure containing the pistil (female parts), anthers (male parts), and surrounding perianth (petals and sepals).

FORM.    Any minor variant or recognizable subset of a species; the lowest category in the hierarchy of botanical classification, *forma;* abbreviated f.

FRUIT.    The seed-containing organ of a plant.

GENETICS.    The science of heredity and variation.

GENUS.    A taxonomic category comprising one or more species of common phylogenetic origin; the hierarchical rank that occurs between the family and species. Plural, genera.

GEOGRAPHIC DISTRIBUTION.    The natural spatial or geographic range of a taxon or group.

GROWTH (SHOOT) HABIT.    The form and relationship of the various parts of the stem and leaves of a plant.

HABITAT.    The locality, site, and particular type of local environment occupied by an organism.

HORTICULTURE.    The art or science of cultivating plants.

HYBRID.    The offspring of a cross between genetically dissimilar individuals, often restricted to the offspring of crosses between species, and showing features of both parents.

INFLORESCENCE.    A cluster of flowers; in *Heliconia* an inflorescence is made up of the peduncle, rachis, cincinnal bracts, floral bracts, and flowers.

INFLORESCENCE BRACT.    A modified leaflike structure, usually boat-shaped and brightly colored, enclosing the flower clusters in *Heliconia* and other members of the Zingiberales; sometimes referred to as a branch bract, cincinnal bract, or spathe.

INFLORESCENCE HABIT.    The orientation of the main reproductive structure; in *Heliconia* the inflorescence can be erect, pendent, or nodding.

INTERIORSCAPE.   The organization and placement of plants in interior, indoor spaces, usually within buildings or rooms.

INTERNATIONAL CODES OF NOMENCLATURE.   Internationally accepted sets of rules for establishing and recognizing botanical and horticultural names, e.g., International Code of Botanical Nomenclature and International Code of Nomenclature for Cultivated Plants.

KEEL.   The central ridge of an inflorescence bract running from the apex to the base.

LABELLUM.   An enlarged, liplike, petaloid structure in the flowers of the Costaceae and Lowiaceae.

LANDSCAPE.   The organization and placement of plants in exterior, outdoor spaces.

LEAF.   The vegetative organ of a plant made up of the petiole and the blade.

LEAF BASE.   The part of the leaf blade adjacent to the petiole.

LEAF BLADE.   The expanded portion of the leaf.

LIP.   The open edge of an inflorescence bract, extending from the apex to the base.

LONGITUDINAL.   Running lengthwise from the apex to the base of a leaf or bract.

MIDRIB.   The prominent central vein of the leaf blade.

MORPHOLOGY.   The form and structure of an organism, with special emphasis on external structures.

MUSOID.   A plant habit of certain heliconias in which the leaves have long petioles and vertically held blades, resembling the shoot organization of bananas.

NATURALIZED.   Successfully established in an area outside the natural range.

NEOTROPICS.   See American tropics.

NOMENCLATURE.   The system of scientific names applied to taxa, or the application of these names.

OLD WORLD TROPICS.    A biogeographic region comprising Africa, Southeast Asia, and the South Pacific; paleotropics.

ORDER.    A taxonomic category comprising one or more families; the hierarchical rank that occurs between the family and class.

OVARY.    The ovule-containing part of the pistil (female organ) of the flower.

PEDICEL.    The stalk of an individual flower.

PEDUNCLE.    The stalk of an inflorescence connecting it to the stem.

PERIANTH.    The two floral envelopes (sepals and petals) considered together.

PETAL.    A member of the inner perianth envelope.

PETIOLE.    The stalk of the leaf.

PHYSIOLOGY.    The study of the normal processes and metabolic functions of living organisms.

POLLINATION.    The transfer of pollen from the anther (male organ) to the receptive area (stigma) of the pistil (female organ) of the flower.

POLYNOMIAL.    A species name that contains more than two words; used before the binomial system was universally accepted.

POPULATION.    A group of organisms of one species, occupying a defined area, and usually spatially isolated to some degree from other similar groups.

PRIMARY GROWTH.    Habitats undisturbed by human activity.

PROXIMAL.    Toward the base.

PSEUDOSTEM.    A false trunk or stem in *Heliconia* and members of the Zingiberales made up of overlapping leaf bases.

RACHIS.    The axis bearing the inflorescence bracts.

RAIN FOREST.    Evergreen tropical forests at middle and low elevations.

RHIZOME.    Underground stem; distinguished from a root by the presence of buds or scalelike leaves.

ROOT.  The part of the plant, usually below ground, that draws water and nutrients from the soil.

SECONDARY GROWTH.  Habitats disturbed or altered by human activity.

SEED.  The ripened ovule, containing the embryo.

SELF-COMPATIBLE.  Able to be fertilized by gametes from the same plant.

SELF-POLLINATION.  Transfer of pollen from anther to stigma of the same flower or to another flower of the same plant.

SEPAL.  A member of the outer perianth envelope.

SPATHE.  See Inflorescence bract.

SPECIES.  A group of organisms that is separated from other groups by reproductive isolation, and that shows recognizable differences from them in color and form; the hierarchical rank below the genus; the basic unit of biological classification.

SPIRALLY ARRANGED.  Many-ranked, with leaves or bracts on many sides of a stem or axis; in *Heliconia* due to the twisting of the rachis.

STAMEN.  The pollen-bearing organ of a plant, composed of the anther and filament.

STAMINODE.  A sterile stamen, often petallike and showy.

SUBSPECIES.  A group of organisms showing only moderate, but consistent, differences from other groups in the same species; the hierarchical rank below the species; similar to variety; abbreviated ssp.

TAXONOMY.  The theory and practice of describing, naming, and classifying organisms.

TRANSVERSE.  Running crosswise from margin to margin of a leaf or bract.

TROPICS.  The geographic region between the Tropic of Cancer and the Tropic of Capricorn; characterized by high temperature, and often by high humidity and rainfall.

TYPOLOGICAL SPECIES. A species defined strictly by the characters of the type specimen without regard to ability to interbreed.

VARIETY. A group of organisms that forms one or more populations within a species, that shows moderate differences from other groups in the same species, and that is often separated geographically from other such groups; abbreviated var.

VEINS. The conducting vessels of the plant body.

VENATION. The arrangement or disposition of veins.

ZINGIBEROID. A plant habit of certain heliconias in which the leaves have very short or indistinct petioles and horizontally held blades, resembling the shoot organization of a ginger.

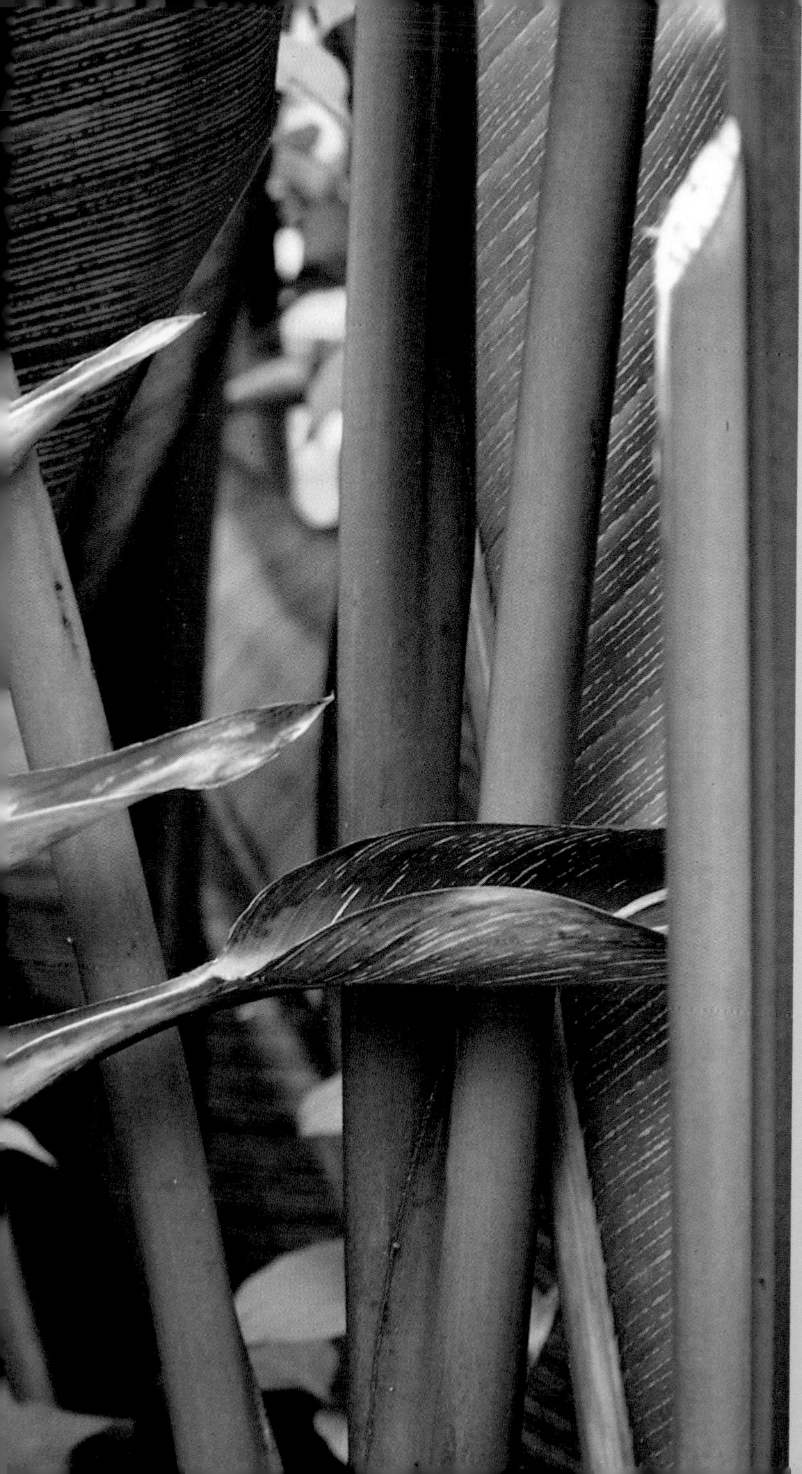

# APPENDICES AND INDEX

# Appendix I.
# Cultivation of Heliconias

*Joseph Fondeur*
*Davie, Florida*

When discussing the cultivation of heliconias, it is important to examine the conditions under which they grow in the wild. Heliconias like water, rich soil, and sunlight. They can be grown in any area where outside temperatures do not go below 40 degrees Fahrenheit for any length of time. Some varieties will show much foliage distress in the form of leaf burn at this temperature. When foliage is damaged from the cold weather all the way down to the base of the rhizome, keep the plant on the dry side and spray with a fungicide. (See section on pests and diseases.) When warm weather returns, the rhizomes will immediately resume their growth. Heliconias that do not grow too tall can be maintained in greenhouses with temperatures in the 60 to 70 degree Fahrenheit range.

PROPAGATION

You will obtain your first heliconia as a potted plant, seed, or rhizome. A rhizome is a subterranean stem, commonly horizontal in position, which usually produces roots below the ground and sends up shoots progressively.

For the beginner, I recommend starting with a potted plant, which will afford you a greater chance of initial success. When your heliconia becomes overcrowded in the pot it is time to divide your plant or put it into a larger pot. (See section on soils.)

To divide: Your heliconia plant can be divided into as many parts as there are rhizomes, but I suggest that you divide your plants into no more than four sections. Insert a large sharp knife or machete into the soil and cut across the soil, making a large X, trying to go between rhizomes. Proceed by taking the plant out of the pot, and cutting the four desired sections cleanly, removing any damaged rhizomes. Now you can plant each section in a pot similar in size to the one the entire plant was in originally.

To repot: Take a knife and run it around the inside of the pot; this will loosen the soil from the edge. Remove the plant, and loosen up the soil at the bottom, to free the roots and allow them to readjust to their new soil environment. Proceed with planting into a larger container.

Planting seeds: Using a very small shallow pot filled with moist soil, bury seeds one-quarter inch under the soil. Keep the soil moist at all times, and maintain the pot in a very sunny and warm area. When seeds sprout, which may take one to twelve months, move them to a less sunny area until plants are mature enough to be replanted.

Planting rhizomes: If you collect rhizomes in the wild or purchase them from a nursery, you should wash them well with soap and water. Rhizomes should be first dipped or sprayed with a good pesticide and then dipped or sprayed with a systemic fungicide. This will reduce the chances of bacterial or fungus growth, which would reduce the chances of the rhizome sprouting. Using the smallest pot that the rhizome can be fitted into loosely, bury it a few inches and place the pot in a sunny and warm place. Rhizomes should sprout in four to eight weeks depending on the time of year.

SOILS

Heliconias thrive in soils rich in organic material. For the best results I suggest the following soil mix for plastic or clay pots. Using equal parts by volume, mix pine bark mulch or pine bark soil conditioner, Air-O-Lite (styrofoam), and Canadian peat moss. To this mixture add one-half cup of lawn and garden lime for every two cubic feet of soil mix (approximately equal to a small wheelbarrow) or one cup per large wheelbarrow (construction type).

At the time of planting, dilute one teaspoon of 20-20-20 soluble fertilizer and ten drops of hormones and vitamins in a gallon of water. Add this solution to your soil mixture until it is soaked. Repeat the solution recipe if necessary, to guarantee soil saturation.

If you are planning on planting your heliconias in the ground I recommend the following: (1) dig the hole at least twice the size of the container that your plant is in; (2) mix the soil (may it be sand, sand-soil, etc.) with pine bark mulch and peat moss in equal quantities and put some of this mixture in the hole; (3) place the plant in the hole, trying not to disturb the soil that surrounds the root system; (4) surround the plant with the soil mixture and press down; (5) water thoroughly.

Because the materials used in the above soil mixture may sometimes be difficult to find, some substitutions can be used when necessary. Air-O-Lite can be substituted with silica sand, sterilized sand, or finely crushed volcanic rock, which will guarantee adequate drainage of the soil mix. Peat moss or pine bark mulch can be substituted with wood shavings (not sawdust, which would pack the soil), rice shells, or macadamia nut shells. It is important to add a greater quantity of these substituted materials because they tend to deteriorate more rapidly than peat moss or pine bark mulch. Sand can be sterilized by baking it for 30 minutes at 350°F, or by washing it with a strong solution of chlorine. After using the chlorine solution, rinse the sand well. Dry the sand in the sun for two days to make sure the chlorine has dissipated.

It is also recommended to always keep the top of the soil mulched. The mulch will deteriorate and fortify your soil.

WATER

Heliconias love water, but they also like the soil to drain quickly. Sometimes we get confused because we see heliconias growing near riverbanks and think they like wet feet. In reality most don't. It is important to remember that river levels rise and lower according to the amount of rainfall. This guarantees that from time to time the soil will have the opportunity to dry.

FERTILIZERS

Heliconias are heavy feeders. The best way to fertilize heliconias is with a balanced soluble fertilizer. Follow the manufacturer's recommended directions, which normally dictate the addition of one tablespoon per gallon of water. This diluted fertilizer should be applied to the foliage as well as used as a soil drench. Fertilization schedules can vary from as often as once a week to a minimum of once a month.

Minor element, or micro-element, spray is recommended three to four times each year as a foliage spray. This will give the plants better leaf color and at the same time will compensate for any lack of iron, magnesium, manganese, or other minerals in the soil.

Granular fertilizers or time-release fertilizers also can be used with heliconias, especially with potted plants. It is recommended that you follow the manufacturer's directions closely. The use of granular or time-release fertilizers is extravagant with heliconias in the ground because many of the nutrients run off when water is applied. Heliconias have a shallow root system, and most of the nutrients will flow away from the heliconias when water is applied to the soil. One way of avoiding this is to drill holes in the soil around the plant and to fill the holes with granular fertilizer.

PESTS AND DISEASES

Heliconias are normally free of pests and diseases, especially if they are grown outside in a very rich soil and are well fed. However, sometimes they will become infested.

The most common pest is the spider mite, and this is especially so when raising heliconias in a greenhouse. These spiderlike arthropods are $\frac{1}{50}$ of an inch long or less, and reddish-brown in color with two black spots on each side. A magnifying glass is needed to spot them. Usually a very fine webbing is seen on the underside or base of the leaves. If detected early, spider mites can be controlled with insecticidal soap. For more persistent cases a miticide must be used.

Mealybugs, white powdery insects about $\frac{1}{10}$ of an inch long, are also attracted to heliconias. To control mealybugs use an insecticidal soap or an oil base insecticide.

Occasionally, snails will chew the young leaves of heliconias, but any slug or snail bait will correct this situation.

A heliconia's worst enemy is fungus. The most common fungi are root rot (*Phytophthora*) and stem rot (*Phythium*). Both of these fungi are preventable with a little precaution. These fungi usually develop when the plants are overwatered or when soil drainage is poor. The growth of fungi can be controlled with any number of general-use fungicides, some of which may also kill bacteria. When starting heliconias from rhizomes, a good preventative method is to dip rhizomes in a systemic fungicide before planting. This is especially true if the rhizomes were collected in the jungle.

As a final note on pesticides, be cautious in their use. Check the label or with the manufacturer to be sure that the specific product has been cleared for application on heliconias. Some products can be harmful to specific types of plants. And always use caution in applying and disposing of chemical pesticides.

# Appendix II.
# Heliconias in Ornamental Design

*Lester Pancoast*
*Miami, Florida*

In the use of heliconias as ornamentals, one can simply select a species, plant it, water it, and observe the response. If inflorescences result, they can then be cut and brought indoors as a cut flower. However, the plants themselves have such beauty, it is sad to leave their entire performance unseen. Civilized people, crowding nature, create their own necessarily limited versions of nature, which they proudly call gardens. Tropical and subtropical gardens or greenhouses can celebrate many kinds of heliconias as their availability increases.

This book can most ideally be utilized by persons with a sense of landscape architecture and design. Any person, however, can make the best use of the different kinds of heliconias by learning their growing requirements, in addition to simple, intelligent culture, and by making the most of the particular characteristics of each.

## SELECTING HELICONIAS

Size, inflorescence characteristics, blooming season, sun and shade requirements, susceptibility to wind and cold, and soil compatibility in the ground or container are all important criteria for selection. A few rare heliconias are difficult for even the best growers; if possible, questions about these plants should be asked of the person who has successfully grown them. If there is no advice, one should experiment! Most gardens have inconspicuous locations for trial and error; trials in containers, when they work, can be brought forward to show or plant. No one selecting heliconias should fail to consider those grown for their exceptional foliage, some of which have relatively insignificant inflorescences.

## HELICONIAS NEED SPACE

A surprising amount of space is required to accommodate a heliconia's propensity to reach upward and outward; without enough space that graceful assemblage becomes a crowded mess which can confuse even a hungry hummingbird. The less nimble human animal needs room to discover, to approach, and to appreciate.

It is not always easy to anticipate how much space a specific heliconia will ultimately claim. A happy, vigorous plant, whether it is contained or not, will in time make powerful attempts to expand, either laterally or centrifugally. The relationship of plant size to the space in which it grows, or to the relative and reasonable size of other plants or features nearby, is a crucial element of landscape design called "scale." A well-grown giant heliconia, twenty-five or thirty feet high, wants a generous, unencumbered space. Such plants are impressive from above or beneath. If the inflorescences are pendent, these can, of course, be seen more easily from below. Smaller plants, down to and including *Heliconia psittacorum*, are closer to the size of a human and present their smaller blooms closer to one's eye. These dwarfs are handsome to look down upon, like most heliconias, but on some other forms the leaves hide the blooms when viewed from above. Others, especially those with higher inflorescences, show well from most angles. Neither dwarfs nor giants, however, should be used where their scale is a problem.

How much ground space do the larger, uncontained heliconias need? Although some varieties may not follow these guidelines, I suggest sixteen to twenty-five square feet for the first two or three years, thirty-six to forty-nine for four or five years, and one hundred or more for six and seven years. Desirable or required ground space or volume of space to contain the leaves will vary, of course, with the species and with the quality of cultivation.

## HELICONIAS NEED PROTECTION

In the same way that any banana plant wants to hide from strong wind, so do the heliconias. Some kinds of heliconias have leaves that divide naturally, without wind; examples are *Heliconia chartacea*, *H. platystachys*, and *H. spissa*. Others are at least graceful at becoming wind-torn; and all seem sensitive to wind-chilling. An open, protected courtyard and an open glen surrounded with dense plantings are ideal places for such plants. Planting near protected water, or even in water for some cultivars (e.g., *H. psittacorum*, *H. marginata*, and *H. rostrata*), can diminish cold damage and reduce growth setback from cold.

## HELICONIAS NEED WATER

These plants are as dependent upon water as upon light, and if not entirely aquatic, like water lilies or lotus, heliconias in nature are often found growing near rivers and streams. The showy bracts and outer leaf sheaths can hold water that is not always creature-free or sweet-smelling, and this tepid broth will readily anoint the incautious. Cutting the stalks of some species releases spurts of water pressurized from within. Heliconias' best visual features create exceptional reflections. The most rigid, unimaginative swimming pool begins an exotic transition when heliconias are brought to it. Informal pools lined with heliconias make one expect that a Rousseau tiger will appear through those leaves to drink from the pool.

Most commercial growers insist that leaves and blooms collected for shipment or display should be cut before 10:00 A.M. in order to capture the greatest amount of stem water, thereby increasing longevity. Some also believe that the deeper the stems are immersed in water, the longer the cut heliconia will last. Give the growing plant or its cut leaves too little water, and those leaves will curl inward to reduce their exposure to dry air or the sun.

## HELICONIAS "WANT TO BE ALONE"

While conceding that they are frequently planted with other plants, sometimes with a vast number of other plants, the designer of a garden should think carefully about which close neighbors will be visually compatible. Even other kinds of heliconias can obfuscate one another, and quite often different inflorescences are not complementary. Colors and forms not strongly contrasting can sometimes startle the habit-prone if matched by sensitive eyes and hands. There are also countless incautious attempts at decoration employed at the expense of heliconias.

Because the human eye must work to separate similar forms, heliconias often combine best visually with plant forms most unlike their own. Hence, poor choices for visual compatibility would be bananalike plants. A better choice would be palms, whose fronds are invariably dissimilar to heliconia leaves. Too many varieties of trees with contrasting forms and leaf textures rapidly make a canopy which will prevent sufficient sun from reaching the heliconias beneath. Even short heliconias planted beneath taller ones must have access to the light they require.

## THE WELL-GROOMED HELICONIA

Growers with experience know that dead heliconia leaves, old stem sheaths, and old stalks which have finished blooming should be removed frequently if the plants are to be healthy and presentable. Such grooming requires access to at least one side of a clump of plants; extensive clumps that are difficult to penetrate are almost impossible to groom. Another problem, that of extensive outward leaning of outer stalks, can sometimes be solved by tying the stems to a central post or to some other nearby support.

## HELICONIAS IN CONTAINERS

Reasons for growing heliconias in containers include the avoidance of unsatisfactory soil conditions and excessive competition from roots of existing plantings, the ease of displaying plants at their best seasons and moving them into protection in case of cold or wind, and the ability to move plants to different light exposures to improve foliage quality or to induce blooming. A strong container with a substantial edge projecting above the soil will help to prevent the "lean-out" problem. However, excessive containment when the plant tightly fills its container can result in an unnatural rigidity if stalks are forced together.

While it takes considerable sunlight and water to grow most heliconias, under the right conditions the containerized plant can be brought indoors to show blooms or greenery for a limited amount of time. Such an indoor visit is most successful when cold and dry conditioned air is not allowed to blow upon (i.e., to cause movement of) the leaves, and when the growing medium is kept damp but not wet; stagnant water quickly rots roots. Depending upon dryness, temperature, and health of the plant, there should be no problem with an almost lightless indoor sojourn of four or five weeks. Cultivars often used indoors include *Heliconia angusta*, *H. psittacorum*, and *H. stricta*, as well as shade-lovers such as *H. metallica* and *H. zebrina*.

Containers limit the grower to plants small enough to be moved. However, there may be circumstances which would suggest moving massive plants in huge containers on rolling platforms or even by means of a forklift. On the other hand, fixed containers can take the form of growing medium placed behind a retaining wall, or of more ambitious infrastructure and architectonics. Either movable or fixed containers, however, bring their own practical and aesthetic problems to be resolved.

HELICONIAS IN THE GROUND

Landscape designers should not look upon heliconias as delicate and temperamental rarities that bring more problems than gifts. In the deep tropics where they are endemic, heliconias are frequently tough, self-perpetuating nuisances that grow in spite of constant clearance. In subtropical places, however, selected varieties can be grown in the ground with little care, replicating themselves for many years even in calcareous soils that are more alkaline than their usual habitat. In more temperate places where frost or persistent cool days or nights prevail, and heated greenhouses are required, container-grown heliconias make better sense.

In the proper places, then, heliconias can be considered as landscape subjects, rather than as special curiosities. The well-grown younger plant with two or three stalks provides an elegant, open silhouette against a wall. The well-grown older plant produces more stalks and more leaves until the wall behind it can no longer be seen, and a series of such plants can provide a rich and full screening.

HELICONIAS AS CUT FLOWERS

The striking color and character of heliconia inflorescences make them much in demand as cut flowers. Unfortunately many types are only being promoted as "special occasion" decorations, in spite of the long-lasting quality of their blooms (two to four weeks). The unfolding of the inflorescence bracts is arrested upon cutting and if refrigerated they will turn an unsightly brown. The "scattergun," eclectic approach to arrangement design involves the collection of several types of heliconia, the tortured cutting of their leaves, and the matching of the inflorescences with countless other flowers, leaves, stems, and unexpected objects. One may sense that I frown upon such behavior, but even I will admit that on rare occasions, when used by the rare individual, such an approach works. The arrangement that requires the greatest skill is the one which has the appearance of simplicity, as in Japanese ikebana, where one, two, or three inflorescences replace a slew of blossoms. This approach is still another art where "less can be more."

Before resorting to strange tricks, it should at least be realized that arrangement of heliconias can be simple. Much more simple if one has heliconia-friendly containers. Substantial, tall, heavy vases that can accommodate at least three stalks of heliconia are perfect, especially if made of glass so the entire stalk may be seen. With straightforward, upright *Heliconia psittacorum*, one needs merely to select a comfortable number of the longest stalks (a few are best cut shorter), remove the leaves, and rearrange the inflorescences behind enough leaves so that a majority of the blooms may be seen. Massive inflorescences that lean heavily outward, such as *Heliconia champneiana* or *H. caribaea,* can usually be balanced in opposite directions. Most blooms are at their best with a leaf or leaves; the leaves of some may last as long as the inflorescences, but only the arranger of long practice will know which. It is curious that the leaves of some forms curl almost immediately upon being cut!

To arrange very large (sometimes several feet long), erect (e.g., *Heliconia caribaea*) or pendent (e.g., *H. collinsiana* or *H. xanthovillosa*) blossoms requires courage and strength. When leaves are simply too large, they must be cut off. There is a special art in cutting leaves at a length and in such a manner that the cutting itself becomes a positive part of the design. Pendent blossoms are best when they hang naturally as on the plant, without appearing confused or crowded, and with their vertical rhythm accentuated. The large uprights can be cut long and used large, or cut very short and placed in a shallow container of water. Dramatic lighting and colorful backdrops can create high design drama in most heliconia displays.

Too few plant-lovers have seen the splendid heliconias in the wild tropics. Those who have develop the urge to add heliconias to their lives somehow. Fortunately more heliconias are now being collected and grown. Today they are more available, more understood, and more widely recognized as valuable treasures for ornamental use than ever before.

# Appendix III.
# Commercial Production of Heliconias

*Richard A. Criley*
*Honolulu, Hawaii*

[Note: Complete citations for those references cited in parentheses with author(s) and date only can be found in "Sources of Information on *Heliconia*." For the other references the complete citation is given in parentheses; "HSI Bulletin" refers to the *Bulletin* of the Heliconia Society International.]

Heliconias are striking plants when used in landscapes, finding use both as accent and backdrop plants and as massed plantings (Watson and Smith, 1974; Watson, 1986). Although heliconias have long been popular conservatory plants, interior plantscapers have begun to use them in containers and interior plantings. Recently, the cut-flower market for heliconias has expanded with much interest expressed by commercial growers in tropical areas seeking crops for export. The intense interest in new potted flowering plants has also led to the development of heliconias as potted plants.

## HELICONIAS AS CUT FLOWERS

In their native regions, even though heliconia flowers may appear in native markets, they have generally been regarded as common and therefore not suitable for home gardens. A few collectors in tropical countries, such as Iris Bannochie in Barbados, Roberto Burle-Marx in Brazil, and José Abalo in Venezuela, have pioneered the appreciation of heliconias. Still, none of these areas has developed large commercial production facilities. The earliest commercial cut-flower production tended to be in areas such as Hawaii and in the glasshouses of Holland and West Germany (van Raalte and van Raalte-Wichers, 1973; Armbruster, 1974).

In the Netherlands, culture of *Heliconia psittacorum* types began in the late 1960s in glasshouses where bottom heating and an air temperature of 25°C were employed. However, the oil crisis of the 1970s increased heating costs to uneconomic levels and forced many growers to discontinue production. Here too, plants were renewed with April–May plantings which came into bloom in seven or eight weeks and kept blooming until low light intensities in the fall reduced quality. A ratio of 1N:2K was recommended (van Raalte and van Raalte-Wichers, 1973). During the 1980s the Aalsmeer Flower Market listed heliconias as the only cut tropical flower besides anthuriums, but volume was small compared to most other cut flowers (Table 1; Ball, HSI Bulletin 4(1): 10, 1989). In 1988, the Dutch auction supply was 591,000 stems yielding a value of 933,000 Dfl (P. M. G. Hendrick, Association of Dutch Flower Auctions, pers. comm.).

TABLE 1.   *HELICONIA* PRODUCTION IN HOLLAND
(D. Ball, HSI Bulletin 4(1): 10, 1989.)

| Species/Cultivar | Stems (× 1000) | | | Price/stem (US$) | | | Season of Sales |
|---|---|---|---|---|---|---|---|
| | 1985 | 1986 | 1987 | 1985 | 1986 | 1987 | |
| *H. psittacorum* | | | | | | | |
| cv. Major | 15 | 26 | 24 | 0.33 | 0.25 | 0.23 | Apr–June, Nov–Dec |
| cv. Pastel | 27 | 39 | 90 | 0.55 | 0.56 | 0.45 | Summer |
| Hanging types | 8 | 2.6 | 9 | 0.84 | 1.70 | 0.96 | Mar–June |
| *H. stricta* | | | | | | | |
| cv. Dwarf Jamaican | 124 | 130 | 190 | 1.39 | 1.19 | 1.07 | Sept–Apr |

A limited approach to commercial cut-flower production of *Heliconia psittacorum* was begun in Denmark in 1986 (Geertsen, HSI Bulletin 4(1): 3, 1989), with four growers involved by 1988 on an area of about 1,000 square meters. The primary cultivar is Tay, which was collected from the Singapore Botanical Gardens, but other psittacorum selections from Florida and the Caribbean area are under evaluation. Cultivar Tay produces 60 to 100 stems per square meter when grown under glass at a minimum temperature of 20°C, with most of this production from June until the light levels drop too low for good quality in the winter. Production of heliconias in containers for interior use is also a good prospect for Danish growers, who are specialists in potted plant production.

In Hawaii, *Heliconia* flower production (Table 2) is year-round for species such as *H. psittacorum,* which are grown in full sun for the strongest stems and highest yields. Plantings set out at 30 cm apart in a row with rows two meters apart can grow into neighboring rows in one year's time. While plantings may be left in the ground more than two years, growers find crowding reduces stem strength and quality even when the tops are cut back to the ground for plant renewal.

TABLE 2.  *HELICONIA* PRODUCTION IN HAWAII
(Hawaii Agr. Statistics Serv., Hawaii Dept. of Agr., 1989.)

| Year | No. Growers | Stems (× 1000) | Wholesale Value (US$) |
|------|-------------|----------------|-----------------------|
| 1985 | 34 | 31 | 125,000 |
| 1986 | 58 | 77 | 391,000 |
| 1987 | 78 | 161 | 1,427,000 |
| 1988* | 83 | 206 | 1,364,000 |

*Estimated production area of 6.6 million square feet.

Other heliconias grown in Hawaii exhibit considerable seasonality in their blooming periods. Some have a narrow season of bloom, such as *Heliconia wagneriana,* which blooms for approximately six weeks from late February to early April. Others, such as

*H. caribaea,* show two cycles of flowering, in March and April and again in September and October. *Heliconia chartacea* produces heavily during July, but scattered flowers can be found in a planting almost year-round, and some growers believe that they can influence flower production through fertilization practices. Many cultivars of *H. bihai* and *H. stricta* are grown as cut flowers and most show some seasonality. Although about a dozen species comprise the bulk of Hawaii's production, there are many named selections and about 20 more species with smaller volumes of production.

In Florida, *Heliconia psittacorum* can be produced outdoors during the warm months from May to November, after which time the temperatures may fall below 10°C. Below 5°C, plants die back and some are killed. Two years is about the maximum time period that a bed should be kept in culture without renewal. A developing shoot requires about nine weeks to bloom during the warm, sunny, long days of summer. High fertilization levels (3.6 kg of 18N-2.6P-10K) produced 130 flowers per square meter in the first year and 160 flowers per square meter in the second (Broschat, Donselman, and Will, 1984). Most of the production recommendations for the *H. psittacorum*-type heliconias have been developed in Florida (Broschat and Donselman, 1983a, 1983b; Donselman and Broschat, 1987).

In the Caribbean area, heliconias and other tropical cut flowers are being viewed as export items for the United States and Europe (Spence, HSI Bulletin 1(4): 8–10, 1986). It is to be expected that the nations where these flowers are native will have a climatic advantage as well as some economic ones (lower land and labor costs), but transportation costs and the presence of native insect pests will pose problems. Thanks to the interest in heliconias generated by the Heliconia Society International, there are many operations developing, but the volume of shipments is still quite low and statistics will be difficult to obtain until the governments involved come to realize the importance of floricultural crops in their trade balances.

In Jamaica, which has had a long history of cut-flower production (anthurium, heliconias, alpinias, bird-of-paradise, roses, and cut foliages), there are new efforts to develop commercial production. It was estimated (Sterkel, 1987) that approximately 150 acres of heliconia existed in 1987 and another 25 were added in 1988 (Sterkel, HSI Bulletin 4(2): 1–4, 7, 1989), with 27 farms cultivating *Heliconia caribaea, H. bihai, H. rostrata, H. wagneriana,* many cultivars of *H.*

*psittacorum,* and the hybrid cv. Golden Torch. Cultivar Andromeda was reported to produce about 160 flowers per square meter, and Golden Torch about 80 flowers per square meter (Spence, HSI Bulletin 1(4): 8–10, 1986). The soils of Jamaica tend to be of limestone derivation, but heliconias do as well here as on the more acid soils of Trinidad. Most operations are located at elevations of 500 to 2,500 feet. An estimate of nearly $4.5 million in cut-flower export had been projected for 1988 until Hurricane Gilbert destroyed large acreages of ornamental nurseries in September of that year. Heliconia operations were projected to be back in operation by late 1989, but the recovery period for other crops will be longer.

High production costs plague producers in Trinidad, which still had fewer than a dozen commercial growers in 1989. Yields of cv. Golden Torch (cv. Golden Bird) approach 150 flowers per square meter, and this cultivar is the most extensively planted one (Spence, HSI Bulletin 1(4): 8–10, 1986). Other species have been introduced and are being bulked up.

In Suriname, a small amount of *Heliconia psittacorum* is being produced, mainly for export to Holland. Only about six hectares are under production in this country, one of the native regions for *H. psittacorum.* In Guyana, many color selections of *H. psittacorum* have been made which have been widely distributed to growers worldwide.

Costa Rica has a well-developed trade in foliage propagules and is rapidly developing cut-flower export capabilities. A 1989 estimate of the value for the principal heliconia/ginger/calathea/cut foliages was about US$1 million, with three-quarters of this going to the United States and the rest to Europe. There are only a half-dozen growers shipping cut tropicals, and the planted area is reported to be about 240 acres, much of which will come into production in early 1990s. *Heliconia psittacorum* and *H. bihai* types are mainly being sold. Although the volume exported has increased, the price per stem has softened somewhat in the past year, and the future must be approached through greater knowledge of the production of competing areas and what the market wants (D. Carli, pers. comm., 1989).

In nearby Honduras, heliconia export existed two decades ago, but a new push is under way to develop heliconias and other cut tropicals for future exportation (D. Tag, pers. comm., 1989).

Elsewhere in South America, interest is quickening, and

the large flower producers of Colombia are evaluating, planning, and planting heliconias for export to the United States and Europe. This area has the potential to outproduce the rest of the world if the growers choose to develop to that extent. Growers elsewhere must keep an eye open for the influx of large volumes of cut tropicals from northern South America and Central America.

In the Pacific and Southeast Asia, interest in heliconias and other cut tropicals has developed with an eye to both American and Japanese markets. Thailand and Singapore already have large export operations for orchids and are looking to add to their export assortment with other tropicals, including heliconias. Heliconia plants are being imported into northern Australia, but no figures are yet available on what portends to be substantial acreages. A small number of heliconias are being produced in the Philippines, Malaysia, and Taiwan, mostly for local use and for export to Japan.

A primary concern of the cut-flower grower is the keeping-life of the product. The large-flowered heliconias look as if they should endure for long periods of time, but often a week is about the best that can be attained before bracts start to turn brown and lose turgor. Even the small-flowered *Heliconia psittacorum* types seldom last more than 14 or 15 days, although ideal holding conditions can extend vase life to three weeks for some cultivars (Broschat and Donselman, 1983b). Flowers last longer when cut at an immature stage (one or two bracts reflexed) than when mature. Local markets, however, often prefer more open inflorescences. Florida researchers suggest that the shortened vase life is due to water stress and the failure of the stems to take up water (Broschat and Donselman, 1983b; Tjia and Sheehan, Greenhouse Manager 2: 94–100, 1984). Floral preservatives were of no value (Tjia, HSI Bulletin 1(1): 6, 1985). One of the research needs for heliconias is improvement of the vase life of the cut flowers.

The original Dutch practice of immersing the flowers and foliage in water for three hours after cutting (van Raalte and van Raalte-Wichers, 1973) is paralleled by the Hawaiian growers' practice of placing all cut heliconias in tubs of water soon after they are cut. In Hawaii's case, the practice is also part of cleaning the flowers and removing insects before they are packed for shipping. Insecticidal dips have been used by some shippers and packers while others use detergents to loosen soil and remove insects. Each inflorescence is cleaned by hand to be sure that it will pass agricultural inspection.

Such practices have kept the quality of Hawaii's blooms high. Exporters of heliconias elsewhere must exercise similar precautions to meet agricultural inspections, particularly in Europe, the United States, and Japan.

Heliconia flowers are exported from Hawaii in large cardboard cartons, layered between sheets of newspaper or packed in shredded newspaper or sleeved in plastic film. A box will often consist of several different species when shipment is made directly to the ordering florists or small wholesale houses. A carton of 20 *H. caribaea* flowers may weigh 100 pounds because a long stem is customary with such large flowers.


HELICONIAS AS POTTED PLANTS

Three species have received most of the attention to date for their potential as potted plants: *Heliconia psittacorum* (Broschat and Donselman, HSI Bulletin 3(4): 4, 1988), *H. stricta* (Lekawatana and Criley, Acta Hort., in press), and *H. angusta* (Ball, 1986; HSI Bulletin 3(2): 2, 1988). In addition, cv. Golden Torch has been used in interior landscape settings in large tubs. Other species may be found usable now that chemical growth retardants have been shown effective on heliconias (Broschat and Donselman, HSI Bulletin 3(4): 4, 1988; Criley and Lekawatana, 1987; HSI Bulletin 2(3/4): 6, 1988; Tjia and Jierwiriyapant, HSI Bulletin 3(3): 1, 6, 1988).

A key to successful potted-plant production is to start with clean planting stock. In pot culture, the limited soil volume often holds too much water and too little air, leading to root and rhizome loss. Field-derived planting stock often carries with it diseases such as the water molds, *Cylindrocladium*, and nematodes. A hot-water treatment (50°C for 15 to 30 minutes, depending on rhizome size) can be helpful in reducing pathogens, especially if a fungicide or surface sterilant is added to the water. Cool the rhizomes immediately after removal from the hot water or they will continue to "cook" inside (Criley, HSI Bulletin 3(3): 6–7, 1988). The rhizome piece and associated pseudostem may be planted directly or held at 20° to 25°C for four weeks to cure and to stimulate bud break and root production. The pieces should be planted with the buds just emerging from the soil, as additional root development occurs at the base of the new shoot. Drenches with fungicides may reduce the possibility of pathogens becoming established.

The potting medium should be well drained, e.g., coarse peat, a mixture of peat and perlite, or a bark:peat:sand medium (2:1:1). The pH of the medium should be moderately acid, about 5.5 (Ball, HSI Bulletin 1(3): 6–7, 1986). Amendments such as lime, super-phosphate, and minor elements may be incorporated into the medium according to a grower's standard practice. As heliconias appear to be heavy feeders, a controlled-release fertilizer may be in-corporated or added as a top-dressing later. A liquid feed supplying 200 ppm N has been used with each irrigation in some pot-culture situations. High levels of potassium do not appear to affect flower quality or quantity (Broschat and Donselman, HSI Bulletin 2(3/4): 5–6, 1987).

Commercial growers dissatisfied with the uniformity of pots arising from rhizome pieces are seeking more uniform planting stock based on tissue-cultured plantlets. Only a few heliconias have been successfully tissue-cultured, and there is no body of research literature presently available for guidance. A three-inch, tissue-cultured stage-4 liner with multiple breaking capabilities is the goal of several labs, which see a future in providing such plantlets to the commercial finishers, much as do producers of chrysanthemum or geranium cuttings.

The control of flowering has focused on several strategies. It was shown that *Heliconia stricta* cv. Dwarf Jamaican responded to short photoperiods by heavy flowering after six weeks of long nights. Later, four weeks was found to be sufficient when the plants were grown at 15°C. At least three expanded leaves were necessary to ensure that the apex had reached a stage where initiation and de-velopment could occur. Development required 13 to 19 weeks from the start of long nights, depending on the size of the plant and the temperature conditions employed. On the other hand, cv. Golden Torch and *H. psittacorum* are not responsive to photoperiod (al-though a recent report from Denmark [Geertsen, Acta Hort., in press] suggests *H. psittacorum* is a short-day plant), but the seasonal flowering of many other species does suggest a photoperiodic con-trol. Many species, including *H. stricta,* have shown flower bud abortion following initiation, which may be the result of tempera-ture or low-light stresses.

Under reduced light intensities, plants of *Heliconia* elongate their pseudostems in competition for higher light intensities. Not surprisingly, this leads to tall plants in the greenhouse. Several reports exist of the use of growth retardants to control height. For *H. stricta* cv. Dwarf Jamaican, the best treatment was with ancymidol at the rate of 0.5 to 1.0 mg a.i./15 cm pot (Criley and Lekawatana, 1987; Lekawatana and Criley, Acta Hort., in press). The hybrid cv. Golden Torch also responded to the same concentrations of ancymidol (Tjia and Jierwiriyapant, HSI Bulletin 3(3): 1, 6, 1988). In both studies, flowering was delayed but not inhibited by the ancymidol, but the retardants paclobutrazol, uniconizole, and flurprimidol have been found to prevent flowering.

A Florida grower is reported to have flowered *Heliconia angusta* cv. Holiday in 15 × 15 cm containers (Ball, HSI Bulletin 3(2): 2, 1988). Plants were grown for a year under 55% shade outdoors in Florida. During their first summer, a gibberellic acid solution (250 ppm) was applied to the foliage. While the plants finished at 60 to 75 cm in height, all did bloom that winter. Many U.S.A. growers are anxious to produce this plant, which normally blooms during the two "red" holidays, Christmas and Valentine's Day.

The principal problems confronting growers of potted heliconias are initial establishment (providing disease-free planting stock and starting environment) and some mite problems. Tissue culture has been suggested as a remedy for disease-infected stock, and tissue-cultured plantlets of cv. Golden Torch were reported to produce side shoots freely (Tjia and Jierwiriyapant, HSI Bulletin 3(3): 1, 6, 1988).

## HELICONIAS IN THE INTERIOR LANDSCAPE

At present, the principal species which have been evaluated for interior landscapes are *Heliconia psittacorum, H. angusta,* and *H.* cv. Golden Torch. These have adapted well to low light although flowering is reduced if the plants are grown their full term under low-light conditions. Others remain to be evaluated and may add considerably to interiorscape potentialities. One which is deserving of such attention is the red and gold flowered *H.* × *nickeriensis.* It has clean, upright foliage with a glossy texture and is about the same size as cv. Golden Torch. *Heliconia latispatha* has also been used effectively as a tubbed specimen.

Suggestions for growers planning to produce plants for interior plantscape use have also been provided (Ball, 1986). Use pots of 20-cm diameter or larger. Establish three rhizome pieces per pot to achieve a large, filled-out look rapidly or begin with well-developed 10-cm pots. Fertilize heavily with nitrogen plus supplemental liquid feeding with minor elements. A pH of 5.5 is recommended for the medium. Plants should be grown at night temperatures of 21°C or higher, as below 15°C growth slows considerably. The higher the light intensity which can be provided, the better; however, some growers will finish plants from the fourth or fifth leaf stage on at 70% of full light to obtain darker green leaves. This procedure gets the plants to a blooming size quickly. If the plants can be installed in the plantscape in bud, they will continue to develop the flowers and bloom for three to four months. If light levels can be held above 350 ft-c, any shoot with five to seven leaves is likely to bloom. On the other hand, low light intensities are believed responsible for the failure of initiated buds to develop (Geertsen, HSI Bulletin 4(1): 3, 1989). While the preceding recommendations were developed for cv. Golden Torch, they apply as well to the forms of *Heliconia psittacorum*.

The variegated foliage forms of *Heliconia indica* are striking in interior plantscape use. Most of these have unattractive bracts and flowers that can be cut off as they appear. Their culture is similar to the large flowering forms, but high light enhances the whites, yellows, reds, and maroons of the variegation patterns.

## SUMMARY

Heliconias offer something new in many ways. They have often been considered as suitable for the botanic conservatory and for "tropical" landscapes, but like many plants, their potential has never been well explored. There are many commercial growers, worldwide, who are discovering the cut-flower, potted plant, and interior plantscape uses of these plants. The potentials of these exotic tropical plants are yet to be fully appreciated by the consumers.

# ndex of Taxa